'Inevitably, we all pass away. Whether the funeral we need to prepare is 2 months or 20 years away, or for ourselves or someone who died leaving no instructions, most of us are at a loss to know what to do. Jeltje slips her hand into yours and accompanies you, step by step, through the process of crafting rituals that honour life and relationships. This guide fills a huge void. It is equally useful for the deeply religious, those who claim no religion and those somewhere in-between.'

– Suzanne P. de Boer, educational consultant for
children with special needs, Modesto, California, USA

'Even young children understand the importance of commemorating a death with others. A friend and I once buried a baby bird that had fallen from its nest. We marked the spot with a lily and precious drops from our ice cream cones. With humility and care, this book brings us back to the authenticity of early funeral rituals.'

– Mia Mohr, artivist with a transatlantic
group of artists, and lives in Talca, Chile

D0707368

by the same author

Crafting Meaningful Wedding Rituals
A Practical Guide
Jeltje Gordon-Lennox
Foreword by Tiu de Haan
ISBN 978 1 78592 390 6
eISBN 978 1 78450 743 5

Crafting Secular Ritual
A Practical Guide
Jeltje Gordon-Lennox
Foreword by Isabel Russo
ISBN 978 1 78592 088 2
eISBN 978 1 78450 350 5

Emerging Ritual in Secular Societies
A Transdisciplinary Conversation
Edited by Jeltje Gordon-Lennox
ISBN 978 1 78592 083 7
eISBN 978 1 78450 344 4

CRAFTING MEANINGFUL FUNERAL
RITUALS

A PRACTICAL GUIDE

Jeltje Gordon-Lennox

Foreword by Margaret Holloway

Jessica Kingsley *Publishers*
London and Philadelphia

Identity icon by © Adaiyaalam CC BY-SA
All other figures, photos and icons © J. Gordon-Lennox
Photos © as indicated

First published in 2020
by Jessica Kingsley Publishers
73 Collier Street
London N1 9BE, UK
and
400 Market Street, Suite 400
Philadelphia, PA 19106, USA

www.jkp.com

Library of Congress Cataloging in Publication Data
Names: Gordon-Lennox, Jeltje, author.
Title: Crafting meaningful funeral rituals : a practical guide / Jeltje
   Gordon-Lennox ; foreword by Margaret Holloway.
Description: Philadelphia : Jessica Kingsley Publishers, [2019] | Includes
   bibliographical references and index.
Identifiers: LCCN 2018058324 | ISBN 9781785923890
Subjects: LCSH: Funeral rites and ceremonies. | Ritual.
Classification: LCC GT3150 .G67 2019 | DDC 393/.93--dc23 LC record available at
   https://lccn.loc.gov/2018058324

British Library Cataloguing in Publication Data
A CIP catalogue record for this book is available from the British Library

ISBN 978 1 78592 389 0
eISBN 978 1 78450 746 6

Printed and bound in the United States

In memory of Michael Picucci, PhD
psychologist, Somatic Experiencing practitioner (SEP)
and pioneer in humanistic ritual as resource

Oh how wrong you are
to think that the years
will never end.
We must die.

Life is a dream,
that seems so sweet,
but joy is all too brief.
We must die.

Of no avail is medicine,
of no use is quinine,
we cannot be cured.
We must die...

We die singing,
we die playing the cittern,
the bagpipes, yet die we must.
We die dancing, drinking, eating;
with this carrion, die we must...

(Anonymous lyrics of seventeenth-century
music known as *Passacaglia della vita*)

CONTENTS

RITUAL TOOLBOX

LIST OF TOOLS WITH THEIR ICONS

★	SEVEN DESTRESSING TECHNIQUES
	Remedies (Smell and touch)
	Hugging (Using touch with others)
	Butterfly hug (Using touch alone)
	Near and far (Eyes)
	Humming (Voice and breath)
	Heavenly drum (Ears)
	Finger labyrinth (Touch)

Pages marked with a 💻 can be downloaded from www.jkp.com/catalogue/book/9781785923890.

FOREWORD

Funerals go back a long way. Evidence of the living burying the dead exists from pre-historic times, accompanied by ever more elaborate associated practices. Central to these was, and is, the funeral. We discover a curious conundrum when we study funerals and memorials over time and across civilizations: the present frequently mirrors the forms and practices of the past yet significant cultural shifts can also be observed at particular points in history (Inall and Lillie 2018). One such shift began in the developed world in the second half of the twentieth century. In Britain, for example, mourners began to express dissatisfaction with the traditional religious funeral, alienated by pronouncements and rites which they found meaningless and a ceremony which provided neither comfort nor a reflection of the person who had gone (Littlewood 1992). In 1980, Barbara Smoker, President of the National Secular Society, set out the purposes of a secular funeral to the UK Cremation Society Conference, including the requirement that it should provide the opportunity for ceremonial and ritual 'leave-taking' of the lost loved one.

Decades later, very few families and friends choose to conduct the funeral themselves (in the way Smoker had envisaged) and a leading UK journalist expressed dissatisfaction with the celebration-of-the-life funerals that have become the twenty-first century norm, describing traditional rituals as, 'infinitely more cathartic' (Coward 2002). The reason for this unease, we discover, is that bereaved families and friends may need help to translate their deepest feelings into words and actions that meet those needs (Holloway *et al.* 2013). It is this void that ritual practitioners, like Jeltje Gordon-Lennox, seek to address.

The notion of the life-centred funeral, in which the funeral address (if there is one) takes the form of a eulogy, is now firmly established in secular culture and has largely replaced theological content in funerals taken by a Christian religious minister. Personalized, customized funerals, with funeral directors keen to facilitate choice and celebrants of all persuasions committed to providing the funeral that the families want in content, style and tone, presenting the person who has died through the recollections of those who mourn them, may seem exactly what contemporary society requires.

What is missing from that description of the modern funeral, however, is precisely the reason why funerals developed and have continued over time and across cultures. It is not remembering *the life lived* with which we struggle, but confrontation with the harsh realities of death. Rite, ritual and ceremony are the tools that human beings have always relied upon to negotiate this difficult terrain, but where religion and social status once provided the framework, participants in the modern funeral must find this, at least in part, for themselves.

Meaning in the face of death is sought, created and taken (Holloway *et al.* 2013) in a creative and dynamic process in which symbols and rituals allow personal meanings to be experienced in a shared public and social act. Traditional sources of comfort may be drawn upon but imbued with contemporary touches – a more diffuse spirituality, including for the holder of religious beliefs; community support received from distant friends of the deceased or sometimes, 'stranger mourners' through social media (Holloway *et al.* 2018). In cultures that favour individualism over community, it is telling that we cannot countenance a funeral without mourners; funeral directors and crematorium staff 'stand in' to obviate such an occurrence. In a recently reported story, thirty people attended the funeral in Orangetown, New York of an older woman, for them a complete stranger, after a young girl found out that nobody was going to attend the funeral and rallied support on Facebook (Warren 2016).

This complexity of emotion, beliefs and context runs through *Crafting Meaningful Funeral Rituals*. Jeltje Gordon-Lennox presents her book as a practical guide for 'amateur ritual makers' – ordinary people who find their day-to-day lives disrupted by the extraordinariness (as it appears for many of us today) of death and do not have the familiarity with ritual to draw on its resources; she also suggests that it might serve as an 'aide-mémoire' for professional celebrants. Although incorporating practical exercises and taking the reader through the steps and task associated with arranging and creating a funeral, this is not simply a 'how-to-do' manual, however.

Gordon-Lennox embeds discussion of each step in the attendant emotions and interpersonal dynamics, weaving together real-life stories from her practice into a funerals narrative that facilitates each reader understanding and creating their own story – their personal 'ritual profile'. This notion is made up of both 'ritual identity' – the individual's identification with particular forms of ritual – and 'ritual practice' – the style of ritual with which the person feels most comfortable. Repeatedly, she asks that we question the purpose of a particular act or use of symbol so that we can tailor it to our own needs. She assures us that a life-centred funeral enables those bereaved to put the life and loss into perspective, whatever the circumstances of the death. Ritual is therapeutic, but it is not therapy.

The funeral is presented by Gordon-Lennox as the opportunity to lay down those practices that will serve the bereaved through the ongoing process of grief. Memorialization is discussed as the 'life after death' – whether that is understood in secular, humanist or religious terms. This is an important addition to the funerals literature that leaves us with the final disposal of the body – the period straight after the funeral long recognized in bereavement research as a lonely and difficult time (e.g. Parkes 1996). Study of memorialization indicates that meaning-making lies at its heart and has always done so. We draw on tradition and past practice, but in the twenty-first century we are seeing a move away from the taking of meaning from handed-down beliefs and practices to the creation of personally customized meanings (Holloway *et al.* 2019). This is what *Crafting Meaningful Funeral Rituals* is all about.

Margaret Holloway
Emeritus Professor, University of Hull, UK

REFERENCES

Coward, R. (2002) 'The problem with grieving.' *The Guardian* (10 April).

Holloway, M., Adamson, S., Argyrou, V., Draper, P. and Mariau, D. (2013) '"Funerals aren't nice but it couldn't have been nicer": The makings of a good funeral.' *Mortality 18*, 1, 30–53.

Holloway, M., Hukelova, M. and Bailey, L. (2018) *Displaying Self: Memorialisation in Contemporary Society*. University of Hull.

Holloway, M., Lillie, M., Dikomitis, L., Evans, N. *et al.* (2019) *Remember Me: The Changing Face of Memorialisation*. University of Hull.

Inall, Y. and Lillie, M. (2018) *Deep in Time: Meaning and Mnemonic in Archaeological Studies of Death*. University of Hull.

Littlewood, J. (1992) *Aspects of Grief: Bereavement in Adult Life*. London: Routledge.

Parkes, C.M. (1996) *Bereavement: Studies of Grief in Adult Life* (3rd edn.). London: Routledge.

Warren, L. (2016) 'Dozens of strangers turn up at funeral for elderly woman after learning no one was attending.' *Inside Edition*. 16 August. Accessed on 7 February 2019 at www.insideedition.com/headlines/18194-dozens-of-strangers-turn-up-at-funeral-for-woman-after-learning-no-one-was-attending

ACKNOWLEDGEMENTS

Write. Leave behind some kind of monument to prove you lived, advised Pliny the Younger (ca. 62–105 CE). Many people contributed directly or indirectly to the writing of this book, including Pliny, whose lucid outlook on life and practical advice to writers appears fresh even today. Although he did not have a publishing team behind him, like me he relied on others to get his texts in shape.

First off, I want to express my gratitude to Natalie K. Watson. Her enthusiastic support lead to the publication of three practical guides on creating secular ritual. The team at Jessica Kingsley Publishers admirably rose to the challenge of making my approach to ritual accessible. After the publication of *Crafting Secular Ritual: A Practical Guide* (2017), which covers six life events or occasions, it was decided that the two main life events in Western societies, weddings and funerals, needed in-depth treatment. *Crafting Meaningful Wedding Rituals: A Practical Guide* came out earlier this year.

Many thanks to the team at JKP for seeing me through yet another book: team leader Emily Badger kept everyone on track, production editor Hannah Snetsinger's amazing patience and organizational abilities always impress me, Helen Kemp's eagle eye took care of copy detail, Alexandra Holmes admirably handled proofreading and publicity executive Lily Bowden gave expert advice. Their close attention to the myriad of details is what turns a manuscript into a book.

Kyle Tevlin, Liselotte Horneman Kragh, Siobhán Cahalan, Anne Berk, Marty Rienstra, Liana Netto, Irene Stengs, Ellen Dissanayake and Matthieu Smyth deserve credit for wading through parts of early versions of the manuscript, as does Sharon Miller who tightened up the questionnaires on ritual profiles. Their pertinent questions and suggestions helped me reflect on my approach and unpack some of my denser ideas.

I would like to express my gratitude to to Albert Bell Jr. for his writings on Pliny and to Margaret Holloway for her visionary work on contemporary funerals and memorials. I am grateful for the support of my colleagues of the European Ritual Network (ERN): Nina Faartoft, Isabel Russo, Tale Pleym, Ida van der Lee, Thomas Wegmüller, Johanna Neussi and Joanna Wojtkowiak. Special thanks goes to Ida for creating public ritual art and to Iben From at the Silkeborg Bad KunstCentret for accommodation. Heartfelt thanks to curator Anne Berk and to my sister Anastasia Aukeman for their artistic vision and their support of me and my work.

Love and thanks to my children, Sushila and Jefferson, for distracting me regularly with their jokes and stories. Above all, I acknowledge Ian's immeasurable contributions to my life, among which is a penchant for detective novels set in unusual times and places such as ancient Rome and modern-day Denmark. This year marks 30 years of mutual support in the pursuit of our respective artistic projects.

PREFACE

No one really wants to have to go to a funeral – much less prepare one. Funerals make us think about the end of life, the death of others and our own mortality. Each one of us has a deeply human story of love and hope, of encounters and disappearances, of life and death. Life has a beginning, a middle and an end. Death represents that inconceivable final chapter. Funerals can help us come to terms, not with death per se, but with the fact that death is part of life. When all is said and done, funerals reflect first of all our relationships to the dead and then the place we give them in society.

TRANSFORMING OUR TIES TO THE DEAD

We like to think of funerals as initiating a process of transformation that allows the bereaved to loosen their ties to the deceased and then, as best they can, reweave the fabric of their daily lives around an irreplaceable loss. Whether and how this happens depends who dies, how they die and on what is now referred to as the 'funeralcare' process.

Twenty years ago, a family called on me to do a conventional religious ceremony for their 96-year-old matriarch. During our first meeting, I learned that the woman had turned her back on organized religion at age 16 – and never looked back. When I asked the family if they thought a religious ceremony was appropriate, her grandson blurted: 'We have to do something! She wasn't a dog!' I reassured them that I would do the funeral but insisted they work with me on a ceremony respectful of the choices the woman had made 80 years beforehand and the values by which she lived.

A conversation with a Buddhist priest revealed that he increasingly finds himself in a similar predicament. People who want to do something but feel estranged from their religion of origin – usually Christianity,

Judaism or Islam – ask him to perform a Buddhist funeral for a non-practising friend or family member. They often want him to preside a 'copy–paste' ceremony composed of a eulogy for the deceased and 'sanitised Buddhist-like texts and rituals' gleaned from the internet.

Figure 0.1. Family gravestone
Located in Boxgrove Priory Churchyard, Boxgrove, West Sussex, United Kingdom.

© J. Gordon-Lennox

In the face of uncertainty, threat and death, human beings feel compelled to do something, usually with or for others, to alleviate their anxiety, fear and sense of powerlessness. This irresistible need to act or carry out a series of actions – even acts radically opposed to the deceased's life and convictions – drew my attention to the number of times I was being asked to perform 'a nice ceremony' (and, sotto voce) 'with no references to god or religion, please'. It also made me keenly aware of how untenable the situation felt to us all, my own family included (see Figure 0.1).

CONFUSION ABOUT RITUAL PROFILE

Many people are confused about what I came to label their 'ritual profile'. This uncertainty leads to muddled 'ritual strategy'. Asking a religious leader for a non-religious funeral makes about as much sense as going to a vegan shopkeeper for eggs or meat. Rather than bemoan the fact that people knock at the wrong door for non-religious ceremonies, I began searching for suitable alternatives. In the process, I became aware that my own ritual profile had changed. Ritual studies scholar Catherine Bell's description of what happened to her resembles my experience:

> Once I was a believer, thoughtfully and intimately committed, and then I was no longer one, with a different set of thoughts and emotions. While I was able to 'explain' my believing and my not-believing in the popular Freudian patois of the day, I wanted to assemble a fuller picture of what had happened and explore whether what was true for me might be useful for understanding others. (C. Bell n.d.)

As a ritual studies scholar, Bell wanted to know what had happened. As a practitioner, I needed to know what comes next.[1] Taking god from the heart of a funeral ceremony felt like a brash, radical and unmapped move. In fact, many scholars still hold that secular ceremonies are devoid of ritual. Convinced that the formerly religious can celebrate their life events meaningfully, I searched for new forms, words and gestures; I even asked myself what one should wear to preside such a ceremony. Journalists soon challenged me with their own questions: Do life event ceremonies performed outside of a religious context count? If so, can they have the power of religious rites? What do these ceremonies look like? What about a wake in a bar or dancing on the beach?

In my efforts to accompany people as they strove to meet their need for

---

1   Batja Mesquita's work on a concept she calls *emotion acculturation* is useful for understanding how one set of thoughts and emotions can be replaced by another set. Experiencing emotions normative to one's subculture is associated with higher wellbeing and lower symptom reporting (Mesquita, Boiger and De Leersnyder 2016).

ceremony without god and religion I learned what it is that makes secular rituals different. Putting the person who has died at the heart of ritual profoundly shifts its focus and purpose (see Figure 0.2). A ceremony that is respectfully centred on the deceased's life, values and relationships can be deeply personal, connect people to each other, remind us of the natural rhythms of life and even mitigate trauma. For this to happen, the setting must feel safe and the ceremony must be planned, created and realized by those who knew the person well. This knowledge unexpectedly led me to develop a creative way to craft new non-religious rituals.

Figure 0.2. Inventor Nikola Tesla's funerary urn
This gilded urn with Tesla's ashes is shaped as a sphere, his favourite geometrical object. It is located in the Nikola Tesla Museum in Belgrade, Serbia.

There are many books about how to die a good death and just as many about how to face illness and mourn (see *Resources*). The aim of this book is to provide a simple hands-on guide to creating secular funeral rituals that honour our ties with the dead. Each chapter opens with a short story and then examines an aspect of a new approach to the practice of art-filled ritual.

If you are pressed for time and eager to begin crafting a funeral ceremony, feel free to skim through Part I, which covers our own mortality and the loss of a loved one. Humans have always understood about death and loss, grief and consolation. By stepping into the past to look at Pliny's views on mortality and his experience of death in first-century Rome, we take a bit of distance from our own fears and anxiety. We see too that a secular approach to ritual is far from new. Part II provides an updated view of contemporary ritual and includes tools essential to the crafting process, such as destressing techniques designed to meet our need to feel safe, notes on how to write up our last wishes and two practical tools on ritual profile and strategy.

Once you determine your own ritual profile and strategy you are ready to move on to Part III, the heart of the guide, where ritual design and materials are discussed. Specially developed tools help determine who or what is at the centre of the funeral, the values to convey through the ceremony and how to transmit them simply and authentically. A checklist keeps you on course and frees you up to fully experience the entire process.

Part IV closes with descriptions of three public memorialization events and reflections on the future of our relationship with the dead. Funeral terminology that may be foreign to many of us appears in a glossary. A short resource section with books, booklets and informative website links is completed with notes on dying and bereavement.

In short, this versatile guide provides the essentials you need to plan, create and realize a funeral that is adapted to your specific situation and context. Those who want recipes for ready-made ceremonies must look elsewhere. 'Ritual is work, endless work. But, it is among the most important things that we humans do' (Seligman *et al.* 2008, p.182).

This guide is designed for amateur ritualmakers, who need to craft a secular ceremony to mark a death. The tools presented here have been forged, tested and tempered with individuals, families and professional funeral celebrants of diverse cultural backgrounds and language groups.

Although it was not originally my intention, I was delighted to learn that the guides also serve institutions in the renewal of traditional religious rites. I may no longer practise formal religion but I admire vital spirituality in all its forms and have great respect for those with devout practice.

The book may serve as an aide-mémoire for professional celebrants, but it is not a substitute for celebrant training. If you are searching for a training course, select one that offers personal attention from a skilled instructor, a mentoring system and the stimulation and support of peers. Online instruction is popular now and useful for studying facts. Learning about ritual accompaniment, how to deal with complex situations and preside at real funeral ceremonies requires face-to-face interaction – just like ritualizing.

MORTALITY

Humankind has always felt the need for ritual.
Part I looks at facing our own mortality and the loss
of loved ones in an ever-changing world. It examines
the purpose and function of funeral rituals.

1

MY DEATH WAITS...[1]

When the buildings all round us began tottering we decided to flee the town. We felt our escape vehicles sway from side to side, even though the ground we were on was perfectly flat. We gaped at the sea as it drew back on itself, as though repelled by the quaking earth. The widening shoreline left sea creatures stranded on dry sand. The sky above us filled with a dark mass of fiery vapour that burst into long, twisting, zigzag flames resembling lightning flashes, only bigger.

Ashes were falling on us more and more thickly. When I looked back and saw a dense black cloud rolling towards us, like a flood that threatened to cover everything in its path, I urged my mother to run. She replied that she was too old, that I should go ahead without her. I pulled her along and said: 'Let's leave the road while we can still see, otherwise we might be knocked down in the dark and trampled underfoot by the crowd behind us.' As soon as we sat down to rest we were enveloped by darkness. This was not the dark of a moonless or cloudy night. This was the blackness of a windowless room when the only light is snuffed out.

We heard men shouting, women shrieking and children screaming with fear. Some called out to their parents, others for their children or spouses; all were trying to pick out familiar voices from the tumult. Howls of anguish rose up around us as people bemoaned their own fate, or that of their near and dear. Some were so afraid of dying that they prayed for death. Many raised their hands to the gods for help. Even more cursed: 'There are no gods, the universe is dying!'

When it grew lighter, we realized it was not the rising of the sun but a sign of approaching fire. The blaze itself actually stopped some distance away, but darkness and heavy ashes fell around us again. We knew that we had to shake them off from time to time or we'd be smothered, even buried under the weight of the ash. Although I'd like to say that, unlike the others, I did not moan with

---

1   The title of this chapter alludes to David Bowie's rendition of Jacques Brel's piece 'La Mort' (1959) which he unveiled in 1972 at his Rainbow Theatre shows (Bowie 1972).

cowardice or cry out from fear, I have to admit here that I derived some poor consolation from my conviction that the whole world was dying with me in this calamity and I with it.

Pliny the Younger (62–113 CE), alias Gaius Plinius Caecilius Secundus, was 17 years old and living with his widowed mother at his uncle and adoptive father Pliny the Elder's villa in the town of Misenum in late 79 CE when Vesuvius erupted, obliterating Pompeii and the surrounding towns. Pliny later became a successful prosecutor and a responsible Roman magistrate, but he is perhaps best known for the great historical value of his collection of private correspondence. This version of Pliny's eyewitness account of his brush with death is adapted from English translations of his letter (LXVI) in Latin to his friend Cornelius Tacitus.

Figure 1.1. Pliny the Younger reproved
As Gaius Pliny the Younger awaits news of his maternal uncle, Pliny the Elder, his uncle's friends scold him for not fleeing Misenum to safety with his mother Plinia Marcella (79 CE).

© *Public Domain. Painting by Angelica Kauffmann (English), 1785, oil on canvas; exhibited in 2016 in Princeton University Art Museum, Princeton, NJ, USA*

FEAR OF DEATH, TRAUMA AND HEALING

Death – whether our own or the demise of those we love – is the ultimate challenge each one of us faces. Pliny held that we do not know what lies beyond death. He would have agreed that the fear of one's own death is more to be dreaded than death itself.

In Pliny's account of how he and his mother survived the fallout from Vesuvius, he remembers his 17-year-old self as having emulated his uncle's calm example. Preferring to read about the past rather than monitor the present situation, young Pliny declines his uncle's invitation to join him for a closer look at the umbrella-shaped cloud rising above Mount Vesuvius. As evening falls, the young man bathes, eats dinner and heads for bed. His resolve to wait for Pliny the Elder's return home does not waver, even when his mother bursts into his room in terror and his uncle's friends warn them to flee (Figure 1.1). Young Pliny's denial of imminent threat is overcome only by increasingly violent quakes that threaten to collapse their house.

FROZEN IN TIME

Although Pliny's vivid narrative reads like a very recent story, the deadly event happened some 25 years earlier. Sensing that there may be more to this young man's cool and collected reactions than his letters to Tacitus reveal, historian J. Donald Hughes writes:

> The fact that [Pliny] tries to portray himself as calm in the midst of storm only protests his own disorientation. His uncle had been calm indeed, but calmness after he had landed at Stabiae only led him to his death. (2013, p.134)

Figure I.2. Roman cinerary urn, ca. 80–120 CE
'The fortunate man, in my opinion, is he to whom the gods have granted the power
either to do something which is worth recording or to write what is worth reading, and
most fortunate of all is he who can do both. Such a man was my uncle,' eulogized Pliny
the Younger (1900, *Letters* VI.16.3). Pliny may have ordered a glass cinerary urn like this
one for his uncle's ashes. Dimensions: 16½ × 9½ × 9½ inches (41.91 × 24.13 × 24.13 cm).
© Public Domain. Collection of the Los Angeles County Museum
of Art, Los Angeles, CA, USA. Gift of Harry Masser

Even without the striking contrast between Pliny's memory of his
nonchalant reaction and his professed shock at the time he wrote about
it,[2] the unusual precision of Pliny's recall is a clue to the young man's
trauma.[3] We now know that the memories attached to an experience

---

2   In response to Tacitus's request, 25 years after the eruption, to know of the terrors and
     dangers of their experience at Misenum in 79 CE, Pliny replies: 'Though my shocked
     soul recoils, my tongue shall tell...' (1900, *Letters* VI.20).
3   Trauma has been and continues to be at the epicentre of human experience (Levine
     2015, p.xi).

that overwhelms the human organism to the point of provoking feelings of utter helplessness, paralysis and imminent death are different from ordinary memories (see Chapter 3).

Pliny was no stranger to feelings of utter helplessness; even before the eruption he suffered the successive loss of his father figures.[4] He was left fatherless at a young age and had several guardians before being adopted by his revered uncle Pliny the Elder, who died from volcanic fallout. As his only heir, young Pliny assumed the funeral duties his family and Roman society expected of him (see Figure 1.2) by giving his uncle a public eulogy. He outlived one or two wives and left no descendants.[5] Pliny's writings reveal symptoms of prolonged, accumulated grief – including feelings of loneliness, guilt and yearning. When he was in his forties Pliny describes his great distress on the passing of another father figure, Lucius Verginius Rufus, at an advanced age:

> I lament his death as though he were young and in glowing health. I lament it – you can consider me a weakling in this – on my own account, for I have lost the witness, guardian and teacher of my life. (1900, *Letters* I.12.11–13)

HARNESSING THE CAPACITY TO HEAL

The traumatized person expends an enormous amount of energy just trying to focus on what is happening in the present. Trauma fragments the mind, traps us in the emotions of the past and even disrupts body functions. Pliny makes no secret of his frail health, delicate frame and weakness of the eyes, throat and chest. While these symptoms may well be related to Pliny's early exposure to volcanic fallout, the last two in particular are often associated with great sadness.

---

4   Modern-day psychological understanding is commonly used now by historians to do retrospective diagnosis of ancient lives. Studying mental illnesses improves our understanding of ancient lives and texts written thousands of years ago (Shapiro 2013).

5   Pliny expressed sadness when he learned that Calpurnia, his adored last wife, miscarried. He has been called 'the first man to write love letters to his own wife' (Sherwin-White 1969, p.79).

What is particularly interesting about Pliny is not his trauma per se but what he felt compelled to do, with or for others, to alleviate his anxiety, fear and sense of powerlessness in order to transform and survive his trauma.

DEFENSIVE SURVIVAL BEHAVIOURS

We know that an experience of embodied action – as opposed to helpless capitulation or uncontrollable rage – is necessary to create an inner sense of control over previously out-of-control sensations and reactions (van der Kolk 2015, p.xviii).

While young Pliny appears to function quite well, evidence suggests that he was a bit of a workaholic.[6] Not only did he survive the reigns of several disparate Roman rulers – in particular the despised Domitian – which was no mean feat, he also managed to rise to the highest administrative ranks in the Roman Empire (praetor and consul). Known for his integrity, acute sense of justice and organizational skills, Pliny was often called upon to sort out difficult situations, including testaments. He kept the affairs of the state, and his own, in good order.

ARTISTIC EXPRESSION

Art-filled activities nourished and nursed Pliny's traumatized spirit. He disciplined himself with physical exercise to enhance his creativity and stay intellectually fit. He also followed his uncle's tireless example and writing habits. Pliny appreciated the theatre and dabbled in poetry.[7] His poems were widely published and he enjoyed reciting them to select gatherings of friends. He was often praised for his eloquent oratory (Hershkowitz 1995, p.168).

---

6   In one letter we find Pliny at his desk during the Saturnalia (the Roman equivalent of Christmas/New Year). In another he refuses to waste time at the chariot races.

7   'For if this little work [poetry] were my chief or sole effort it might possibly seem unkind to tell me to "find something else to do": but there is nothing unkind in the gentle reminder that I *"have* something else to do"' (1900, *Letters* IV.14, cited in Hershkowitz 1995, p.168).

EMOTIONAL GRANULARITY[8]

Pliny wrote that his literary activity brought him 'joy and comfort; it increases every happiness and consoles every sorrow' (cited in A. Bell n.d.). The careful rigorous style of his missives was admired as a miniature art form.[9] His emotional vocabulary expanded as he composed these stylized private letters to inform his friends and colleagues of public and private happenings in the heyday of the Roman Empire.[10] Pliny kept notebooks at hand even on hunting trips so that, if there was no game to be had, at least the time and the inspiration of the countryside would not be wasted.

ALLEVIATING OUR FEAR OF MORTALITY

Many of Pliny's tactics for lessening his sense of powerlessness in the face of mortality are examples for us. We too can work to stay fit, practise various forms of artistic expression, consciously expand our emotional vocabulary and keep our affairs in order.

The majority of Britons, aged 18 and over, polled online in 2010, indicated a preference for a personalized celebration of their life (Field 2011). A study of Australians, aged 50 and over, took it a step further and asked people what *tone* they would want for their funeral. The majority (59%) would opt for a relaxed and reflective funeral, 27 per cent chose a jubilant/fun/celebratory funeral and a mere 1 per cent preferred solemn and serious (McCrindle 2014).

---

8   Psychologist Lisa Feldman Barrett holds that people who cultivate finely tuned feelings or 'emotional granularity' are better at regulating their emotions and less likely to drink excessively when stressed or retaliate aggressively against someone who hurts them. They may also have longer, healthier lives, go to the doctor and use medication less frequently, and spend fewer days hospitalized for illness (Barrett 2017, p.106).

9   Pliny's private letters are carefully written, occasional letters on diverse topics. Each has a single subject and is written in a style that mixes, in Pliny's terminology, the historical, the poetical and the oratorical manner, to fit the theme. The composition of these litterae curiosius scriptae (letters written with special care) was a fashion among the wealthy, which Pliny developed into a miniature art form (Encyclopaedia Britannica 2018).

10 His letters to his last wife Calpurnia, written near the end of his life, show how his expression of emotion evolved.

Surveys of the bereaved tell a different story: only 1 per cent of Britons preparing a funeral admitted to knowing all the deceased's funeral preferences, with 31 per cent having no idea whether their loved one would have wished to be buried or cremated, and 53 per cent uncertain about whether to hold a religious or non-religious service (SunLife 2015). Although having your goodbye ideas down on paper, in your own handwriting, is an indisputable document of what you want, there seems to be a widespread reluctance to put it in writing. Only 6 per cent of the Australians interviewed had left their last wishes with a funeral director.

The discrepancy between what people say they want and the provisions they make explains why some 67 per cent of the funerals registered by directors of 850 funeral homes in Great Britain still take a traditional form, that is, a ceremony with religious rites lead by a religious leader, followed by burial or cremation (Field 2011).

The increase in desire for a non-religious funeral along with the receding influence of institutional religion have purportedly left a ritual void that some celebrants and funeral directors propose to fill with a repertoire of 'traditional' ceremonies. What does it mean to have a traditional funeral? Does it involve replicating a cultural practice, tweaking a religious rite or doing what most people in town do?

Participants in an innovative study asking open-ended questions about how people feel about the traditional funeral describe it as being like a lonely, lifeless tomb: suffocating, confining, cold, sterile, lifeless and dark. They observe that family and friends remain sad, lonely and disconnected after the service (Funeral Service Foundation 2012). Whatever the traditional funeral is, it is a far cry from what the majority of Australians – the 86 per cent who opted for a relaxed, fun funeral – are thinking they might get (McCrindle 2014). Kyle at iwantafunfuneral.com says: Why gamble on your friend's and family's collective memory when it can be so easily assured with a pen and paper?

Before turning our attention from our own mortality to that of those close to us, take time to arm yourself against the strain of funeral preparation by learning a few simple destressing exercises (see *Seven destressing techniques*). Prepare for the inevitable by writing out what you want for your funeral. Notes on last wishes give practical advice on how to get the kind of funeral that best suits you.

Behind the scenes...

The artists featured in this chapter show how feelings about the mystery of death can be channelled into artistic expression. The title is a nod to David Bowie (1947–2016) who flirted with the taboos around death throughout his career. By all accounts, he considered himself a near atheist who was in awe of the universe and fascinated by ritual. Bowie's own death waited on his birthday, and the release of his oeuvre ★. *Blackstar* was his last salute to his fans; it signalled the end of his youthful career and anticipated his death two days later. The adventures of Pliny the Younger, an atheist and artist in his own right, inspired historian and writer Albert Bell Jr. to put him at the centre of a series of murder mysteries set in Rome during the late first century of our era. Both Pliny and Bowie made advance plans for their funerals.

 ## NOTES ON LAST WISHES

The provisions of Pliny's will were practical. They included money for upkeep of the public baths in Como and a good supply of soap. Pliny delivered the eulogy for his uncle in a traditional Roman ceremony. In view of his wealth and rank, he most probably had a similar funeral. Pliny left a will. He held no illusions about the good intentions of the living; even the most loyal friends may neglect the wishes of the dead.

In most countries, people can make one or more legal documents that specify what actions should be taken if, for any reason, they are no longer able to make decisions for themselves regarding their belongings, body and being. In the United States, a will has a legal status and may also cover funeral arrangements. In France, laws protect funeral plans. The family can be fined or jailed if the deceased's wishes for the funeral are not respected.

Last wishes documents should cover three main areas: provisions for *belongings* and people (the will), for health and *body* (living will) and for *being*, for example, funeral and last resting place (Coronach[11] will). These documents must be drawn up while you are still legally fit to do so. It is an act of love and respect for loved ones to put in writing what you want to happen and who should be named responsible if you should become unable to decide about your health treatment and property (or debts). Once your wills are written up and signed, make them accessible[12] and reapprove them every few years. Some countries require witnesses.

THE WILL

Setting up a will is usually not that difficult or expensive. Consult an attorney or a solicitor to evaluate your testamentary requirements. Transparency with loved ones saves hard feelings at the end. Tell your family what you want to do, the content of your will and where to find it. If you intend to leave money to charities, explain what it means to you to be able to do so. Parents of underage or disabled children are strongly encouraged to designate people they trust to raise their children in their stead.

---

11 All cultures borrow or invent new words to give language precision and emotional granularity when the existing ones fail to describe new practices or attitudes. The Scottish Gaelic word *coronach* is composed of *comh-* 'together' + *rànach* 'outcry'. It denotes the (angry) outcry of a group against the death of a loved one through a very personal and spiritual Scots practice. See the painting *A Coronach in the Backwoods* (Simson 1859). At the beginning of the sixteenth century, the word appeared in English to refer to funereal lamentations and dirges sung or played on bagpipes. It is reintroduced here to call attention to the personal and spiritual practice of preparing certain essential elements in advance that pave the way for mourner's meaningful outcry against death.

12 Living and coronach wills that are opened only *after* your funeral will be rather useless.

WHO KNOWS YOUR PERSONAL CODES?

What happens to our 'digital assets' when we die? All our ID codes and passwords for various electronic devices, as well as credit cards and bank accounts, are supposed to be kept secret, right? It is prudent to keep your codes, especially those for mobile phones, in a closed envelope in a safe place that is accessible to the person who assumes responsibility for your funeral to be able to notify your friends of the date and place. Facebook, Twitter and Instagram accounts and email addresses should also be considered part of your assets.

LIVING WILL

The living will, also known as advance healthcare directive, personal directive or human document, was developed in the 1960s in reaction to the escalating sophistication and expense of medical technology. In most places a living will gives people the right to formulate advance instructions as to what type of healthcare they would like or refuse, and to designate a trustworthy surrogate decision-maker to step in if they are no longer able to to express their will. Check with your family doctor about the laws in force in the country where you reside or travel regularly.

Recent counsel about advance directives tends towards asking open questions about a person's personal values, rather than focusing on specific treatments and medical procedures (see also *Resources* for *Notes on mortality, death and dying*).

- What do the terms 'life support treatment' and 'comfort care' mean to you? When would you definitely want or not want it? Would painkillers that might hasten your death be acceptable to you?

- What are your personal grooming, bathing and feeding instructions? How do you feel about touch or massage with oils? What about tube feeding if you show no signs of being hungry?

- How do you want to be treated? What kind of accompaniment do you want, or not want? Who do you choose to have, or not have, at your bedside? How do you feel about being cared for at home, in a hospital or in hospice care?

CORONACH WILL

Whether out of of diffidence, negligence or superstition, death and funerals are subjects one does easily not broach with one's parents, partner, children or friends. There is one funeral I will never forget. Shortly before I stopped doing religious ceremonies, the administrator of a nursing home contacted me for the funeral for an elderly woman. There was little information about her life so it was basically a liturgical ceremony. As we stood around the open grave in a small group, a cousin who had just arrived from Corsica announced: 'Her husband was athe ist. He had a humanist[13] ceremony and was then cremated. I'm sure she wanted that too.'

In the end, the nursing home representative spoke up: 'Her intake file states no preference for any particular kind of funeral, nor does it specify burial or cremation.' The funeral director nodded, and the gravediggers lowered the casket into the ground. The tool for drawing up a coronach will is found in the toolbox for the preplanning phase (Chapter 4).

---

13   Humanist traditions reflect a positive attitude towards life, based on human experience, respect, responsibility and hope. Humanists believe that only through experience and rational thinking can one find a pathway to knowledge and also a moral code by which to live.

2

GONE TOO SOON[1]

'Vanessa, is that you?'

'Hey Jake, good to hear your voice.'

'Where were you and Kerry last night? The Masses concert was great! You never showed up. Didn't answer your phones either...'

'I'm in hospital, Jake.'

'What!?'

'We were on our bikes, on our way to meet you. Kerry was saying something silly about an ubergoth she saw last night. This big truck...blew us off the road, Jake. Drove off... Tangled metal... Somebody called an ambulance...'

'Vanessa! Are you there? How are you?'

'Broken leg and arm, concussion... Was lucky.'

'Lucky?! Where's Kerry?'

'Kerry...didn't make it, Jake.'

'I'm on my way.'

'Bring everybody, Jake. Anna, Kerry's mum, is in rough shape. Her Dad's still in China. Probably not coming...'

Anna feels caught between the needs of two different generations: Kerry's friends' eagerness to do something is clouded by their initial disorganization. Kerry's grandparents insist on a socially acceptable funeral. The funeral director urges Anna to opt for formal obsequies that she will not regret later. Finally, Anna agrees to a 15-minute public ceremony presided by crematorium staff.

Four days after Kerry's death, an officiant greets a small assembly gathered in the chapel. She reads the poem 'Life' by Charlotte Brontë before introducing the music chosen by Kerry's family: 'Gone Too Soon' by Michael Jackson (Kerry's father), Celine Dion's 'Fly' (maternal grandparents), 'If I Die Young'

---

1   Refers to the title of a ballad recorded by Michael Jackson; it appears on his album *Dangerous* (1991).

by The Band Perry (Anna and Merry, Kerry's 12-year-old sister). Between the songs Kerry's paternal grandfather reads a note from his son, an aunt says a few words. Jake then invites everyone to a memorial service that will be held when Vanessa is out of hospital. After the ceremony, close family share a light meal at Kerry's uncle's home.

Three weeks later, Jake, Vanessa and their friends hold a nighttime ceremony for Kerry in the courtyard of the squat where Jake lives. Nearly 300 people attend, including both of Kerry's parents, her sister, a grandmother and a few aunts, uncles and cousins.

The mourners are welcomed with 'Exit-Gardens' by the Austrian group Whispers in the Shadow. After Jake greets everyone, Anna and Merry enter the ceremonial space carrying the urn with Kerry's ashes to the music 'Seeing You Here and Now' by Rosegarden Funeral Party. Several people speak about Kerry and what she meant to them. The ceremony ends with 'Left Behind' by the Australian group Masses. The evening continues with the goth music and industrial dance that Kerry loved. A caterer hired by Kerry's father serves his daughter's favourite foods (spaghetti, fresh veggies and chocolate cake) and non-alcoholic beverages.

In small groups, they speak about Kerry, and also about death. When asked what he thinks about his own death, a 22-year-old man in full goth[2] attire exposes his blackened teeth, smiles and replies: 'I don't.' His white-faced 18-year-old girlfriend cuts in: 'I'm terrified of death. Kerry's death makes me even more scared of dying. I don't ever want to die.' A black-caped 40-something woman with blood-red hair swivels her scythe in time to the music and adds: 'We goths have a romantic nineteenth-century fascination for dark things. We laugh about death. It's a creative way of handling the fear of losing those we love, our own death and being dead' (see Figure 2.1).

Shortly after midnight the police stop by to ask the group to turn down the music and the crowd slowly disperses.

---

2   Goth music, with its typically nightmarish themes, violent lyrics and a dark musical ambience, opened the way for what was considered a negative subculture in the 1970s. David Bowie had a definite impact on early goth subculture. Seminal bands like Siouxsie and the Banshees, Bauhaus, The Cure and Cabaret Voltaire are sometimes called his dark children. A shift occurred in the goth scene in the early 1980s in London when it acquired a more positive identity. Goth genre has spread to urban areas around the world. In addition to film and music, goth now includes taste in aesthetics, art, fashion and even lifestyle (see Figure 2.1).

Figure 2.1. The grim reaper
Goth woman poses as the Grim Reaper, a mythical figure that personifies Death. Nearly every culture has stories of how such a figure – usually a scythe-wielding woman, man or skeleton in a black cape or shroud – visits the living to announce their death or to collect the dying.

© Lars Plougmann, CC BY-SA

During those first emotion-filled hours and days after the death of a loved one, mourners often feel isolated by their grief. Sorrow is a physical experience that transforms slowly, often in fits and starts, into a conscious realization of loss. Time and place become irrelevant. The bereaved may speak of the dead person in the present tense, then use the past tense, and return again to the present. Ties to the deceased seem to intensify, while relationships with the living may be weeded out. Lives are turned upside down and tempers are short.

Yet the next of kin are expected to make what often feels like premature decisions to get the funeral (read: corpse) out of the way. Our culture is simply not geared to letting people emerge at their own rate from the shock of loss (see Figure 2.2). As we saw in the last chapter, a majority of the bereaved either have no clue about what to do or they do not agree among themselves. It is no wonder putting together a funeral can be such a challenge – and the result too often disappointing.

These quandaries illustrate the confusion today about the purpose and focus of funerary rituals.

Figure 2.2. Victorian post-mortem portrait of an infant
Post-mortem photographs of a beloved child helped Victorian parents mourn and remember. Often these pictures were small enough to to slip in a pocket or a locket. Years later, the life-like image of the child could be held in a hand, stroked, talked to, kissed and cried over.

© *Public Domain. Portrait of a mother with her dead child*
(ca. 1860–1900). Property of the National Library of Norway

Barriers to a fitting funeral

When the deceased is not a card-carrying member of a religious or humanist institution, the hurdles to a meaningful funeral multiply quickly. Just to be clear: these obstacles are *not* due to a lack of faith or lapsed membership.

The three main barriers to meaningful obsequies are:

1. *Social pressure* to treat death as a disagreeable happening that must be dealt with as quickly and unobtrusively as possible.
2. *Turnaround rates* in the funeral business. In one to five days, tops, bodies are moved from a medical establishment to the morgue to the cemetery – with or without a short pause for a ready-made ceremony.
3. *Lack of advance planning* on the part of the deceased.

The first two hurdles can be jumped over by settling for a private cremation[3] or burial, followed by a public memorial service in a place the deceased cared about, at a date and a time convenient for the chief mourners. The third obstacle is more problematic. Just as one must be measured for a custom suit, a tailor-made ceremony also requires taking certain measures.

WHAT ARE FUNERALS FOR?

Think back to the last funeral you attended. If you have never been to one, call to mind a funeral portrayed in a film or on television. Who or what was at the centre of the ceremony? What happened? Was the casket present? Was the body shown? Was the person who presided a religious or secular

---

3   Cremation, which began as a trend in Western society, now appears as a long-term solution. It is cheaper than burial, seems 'cleaner' and opens the way to a wider range of rituals that are not contingent on the funeral parlour nor legal delays for disposal.

leader, a family member or a friend? Did you recognize the person you knew in the way the ceremony was handled? If the funeral was not centred on the deceased, if you did not learn something new about this person's life, or how she or he died, you probably came away feeling a bit cheated.

The purpose of a funeral is four-fold:

DISPOSING OF THE BODY

The rude transition from body to corpse implies certain legal conditions, restrictions and obligations, all of which involve disposal. The most common practices include variations on burial such as inhumation (in the earth), immurement (in a mausoleum) or a sea burial, cremation, exposure to the elements or to scavenging animals or birds (known as sky burials) or dissolution (in a solution or acid).

Direct disposal[4]

In view of rising funeral costs and the difficulty in organizing a fitting ceremony, the bereaved may opt for an alternative to the conventional funeral known in the funeral business as 'direct disposal' or a 'direct funeral'. It meets legal requirements for dealing with a corpse and is by far the cheapest plan. Under certain circumstances, it may be the only realistic or humane solution.[5]

Like public health funerals (also called pauper's funerals) direct funerals are no-frills services. No provisions are made for flowers, viewings, obituaries, funeral processions, a hearse or transport for family members. On a day and time determined solely by the undertaker, the corpse is transferred directly from the medical facility to the crematorium or the

---

4   The number of public health or pauper's funerals recently increased by 12 per cent in Great Britain (Morely 2018). Thousands of people, mostly elderly, have no family or friends to care for them or to arrange, attend or pay for their funeral; some families simply cannot afford one. Claims that some public figures such as John Lennon, Anita Brookner and David Bowie chose direct disposal may simply be a ruse to protect their need for privacy, or hype for the service.

5   When someone dies abroad and their family wants to take the remains back to their home country, direct disposal is often the most practical option. If this is your case, make sure the procedure complies with the laws of the country the urn will be travelling to and from, as well as the carrier's requirements (transfer by airline, train, boat).

cemetery, with no stopover for a ceremony or a few last words before the disposal. In fact, if even one person is present at the crematorium or the gravesite it is not considered a direct funeral.

Regardless of the reasons for the choice, the ramifications of such a decision should not be easily dismissed. Once dead, the human body is an object, a corpse that is both a person and a thing. As a person, this body-corpse is material evidence of a multitude of relationships and identities: my mother, his wife, their child, her friend, his mentor or the next-door neighbour. Each one of these relationships is proof of a certain continuity of what used to be a living being. These ties deserve to be honoured (see Figure 2.3). Although direct disposal makes no provision for a funeral, there is no reason not to hold a farewell ceremony before disposal (without the body) or to arrange for a memorial ceremony at a later date (with or without a cinerary urn).

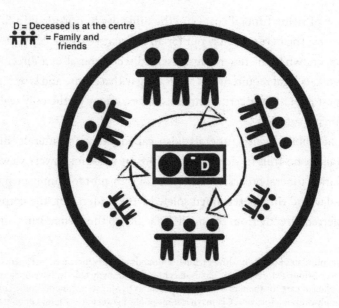

Figure 2.3. The funeral
Death represents the end of life but also the end of physical ties with family and friends. These relationships are at the centre of a meaningful funeral. The closest family members and friends are represented in this drawing by the larger figures and the other participants at the funeral by the smaller figures.

TAKING LEAVE OF THE DEAD

In Western societies it is commonly held that funerals are for the comfort of the living.[6] This assumption is understandable, particularly since they must organize and often pay for the funeral. Too often, however, this means that whoever pays the piper calls the tunes.

Some years ago, my husband and I attended the funeral of a close friend, Marie, who had openly rebelled against her parents' strict religious upbringing. Marie's partner and their daughter were overwhelmed by her sudden death. Undoubtedly motivated by good intentions, Marie's parents publicly announced there would be a traditional religious funeral four days after their daughter's death. The setting and content of the ceremony were distressing for Marie's partner, their daughter and their friends. The only moment that felt meaningful to us was when her partner, an accomplished professional musician, played a piece Marie loved while their daughter silently turned the pages of the score.

Under what appears to be similar circumstances, I accompanied Susana, a recent widow, and her son Claudio, as they crafted a funeral for Paulo, a middle-aged non-religious man who died after a short illness. Susana and Claudio were concerned that Paulo's mother, an aged and very religious woman, would not appreciate the kind of funeral we were planning. As I observed Paulo's mother during the ceremony, she seemed captivated by the stories people told about her son. At the reception, Susana smiled when I asked her what her mother-in-law thought of the ceremony. 'I don't think she even realized it wasn't religious. She just told me: "You know, it must have been Paulo's time. Hearing all those people talk about my son, about all he'd accomplished, made me feel proud."'

In both situations, a parent died prematurely, that is, before their own parents and while their children were still quite young. Who were

---

6   The position that funerals are for the living rather than the dead is closely tied to the rise of monotheistic religions, humanism and consumerism. Religious scholars, notably Augustine and Calvin, and scientists alike, distanced themselves from animistic practices by encouraging mourners to pay little heed to the the dead. The view that funerals are for the living is perpetuated in the twenty-first century by religious, funeral and bereavement professionals. Chief mourners, however, tend to remain focused on their relationship with the deceased (Chapter 8).

the funerals for? Marie's funeral was for her parents and about their ritual tradition. Paulo's ceremony was for and about him. Funerals are essentially carried out by the living but they are performed for the dead. The dead need funerals and the living need poignant funeral rituals.

Funeral rituals are meaningful to the living when they can recognize the deceased in the ceremony – and have no regrets about the decisions made. Being clear about ritual profile is the first step towards a suitable ritual strategy. It gives direction to the creation of a ceremony or memorial service and ensures that it reflects the different facets of the deceased's life, values and relationships (see *Inventory on ritual profile for funerals*).

SUPPORTING MOURNERS

A fitting funeral gives family and friends an opportunity to say goodbye in a place that feels safe and supportive to them. Nearly half the UK population, a third of people in the United States and Canada and a quarter of all Australians now classify themselves as 'nones' (popular shorthand for atheists, agnostics and the non-religious). This shift has resulted in an 80 per cent rise in secular funerals in the United Kingdom over the last few years (Telegraph Financial Services 2017). Religious send-offs are increasingly replaced with celebration of life ceremonies in North America and Australia too.[7]

As in Kerry's case, older relatives may consider a celebration of life irreverent or even offensive, while contemporaries of the deceased often find a traditional ceremony irrelevant or upsetting. Inappropriate funerary rituals can hamper mourning because they divide rather than draw people together. The humanizing effect of a meaningful ceremony should not be underestimated. Marie's family distorted the image of their daughter's life, eroding any mutual comfort the assembly might have gleaned from the ceremony. Since Paulo's funeral focused mourners'

---

7   Statistically, the United States and Western European countries have a broadly similar religious makeup. When it comes to belief and practice, however, the differences are striking. Both religious and unaffiliated US adults are considerably more religious than their European counterparts (Evans 2018).

attention on him, the assembly – including his religious mother – could support each other in their shared loss.

Rituals that make sense provide a safe framework for expressing and harnessing strong and potentially dangerous emotions in a harmonious and fulfilling manner. Ritual that feels right and trauma resolution make use of the same innate capacity to rebound following an overwhelming experience. This potential, which is biologically linked to an animal-like surrender to the sensate world within, can awaken our life force (Levine 2010, p.256). As authentic ritual connects us to our senses, it grounds us and contributes to healing, as well as to the prevention or renegotiation of trauma.

BENCHMARKING SEPARATION

As a funeral celebrant, I observe that the attention span of the assembly is short. People do not stay long with an emotion; they spontaneously oscillate between pain and pleasure.[8] Tears and laughter may follow in rapid succession. An overwhelming sense of absence may be replaced by a joyful memory, followed by the unacceptable sight of their loved one in a coffin, and then the warm comfort of a friend's hand... When the ceremony flows in a gentle, harmonious manner, people feel supported in the unthinkable transformation of the body of their loved to a corpse. The words and gestures that substantiate separation may give rise to signs of physical release or discharge: a deep breath, moist eyes, yawning, a trembling in the face, lips or hands, and movements that stretch muscles in the shoulders, neck, hands or legs. As the ceremony draws to a close, people glance around, as though they are waking up and reorienting themselves to the room and the people around them. They move less stiffly; their faces soften. The end of the funeral serves as a benchmark or reference point among a series of lesser points in the grief process.

---

8   Although biophysicist Peter A. Levine never directly applied to funerals the oscillation he prescribes for the resolution of trauma, he observes that 'the tranquil feelings of aliveness and ecstatic self-transcendence that make us fully human can also be accessed through ritual. This way they become enduring features of our existence' (2005, p.xvii).

ABSENCE THE GREATEST PRESENCE[9]

Later, mourners may speak of a gut-level sense of relief or tranquillity. They have moved to new place in their grief. A place where they live without their loved one's physical presence but can still feel close to her or him. Funeral rituals are meaningful when they are consistent with the deceased's values and life. Meaningful funeral rituals are for the living and the dead. They contain the emotions of the past in the past, and firmly anchor people physically and sensorily in the present, thus opening the way for a new future.

Behind the scenes...

In ancient Rome, the ephemerality of life was an accepted fact. *Memento mori*, an obsession with last wills, numerous monuments to death, gladiators fighting to the bitter end and philosophers who argued that any day might be one's last all suggest that death and the dead were close neighbours to the living, neighbours that were to be confronted rather than shunned (Hope 2009, p.17). A family's obligation to dispose of the dead body set them apart from non-mourners as well as from the corpse. 'Usual expectations were reversed and sensory experiences turned on their head' (p.122).

> [T]he corpse was tidy and clean, the mourners dishevelled and dirty; the corpse wore pale clothing, the mourners dark; the corpse was silent, the mourners noisy; the corpse was motionless, the mourners could move often and rapidly; the corpse was perfumed, the mourners were unwashed; the corpse could be offered food and drink, the mourners may not have eaten. (Hope 2017, p.95)

Victorian era mourning rituals included condolence letters, listening to elegiac poetry, visiting graves, wearing fashionable Victorian *memento mori* jewellery, made from the dead loved one's hair, and

---

9   Attributed to May Sarton (1912–1995).

death portraiture. As articles to be touched, carried and wept over, these objects represented nurture, connection and love.

Today's equivalents include synthetic diamonds made from the deceased's ashes or a small stainless steel capsule with their DNA, the return to funerals at home and photographs of the dead seated once more on his motorcycle or smoking her last cigarette. As direct disposal becomes more popular, the number of conventional funerals decreases. This shift is due, at least in part, to a certain confusion among the next of kin about the purpose and focus of a funeral and the growing desire to ritualize leave-taking outside the traditional institutions associated with death and funerals.

NOTES ON RITUAL PROFILE AND STRATEGY

Before making arrangements for any funeral – your own or that of a loved one – sort out ritual profile. Accurate assessment determines which ritual strategy will be the best for a particular funeral. Appropriate ritual strategy makes the difference between a ceremony that feels right and a failed funeral.

Traditional surveys based on affiliation to institutional religions are ill suited to track ritual practice today. We need new tools and categories that measure not just official religiosity, or lack of it, but ritual profile. In Switzerland, an urbanized country with four language groups and a unique position at the crossroads of Europe, changes in the religious landscape are studied closely. A government-funded project (Stolz *et al.* 2011) based on the last few census reports uses broader and more inclusive categories than most demographers. The question sheets proposed in this guide expand the Swiss profiles beyond affiliation and religiosity to take into account ritual profile and practice (see the following box with ritual profiles).

RITUAL PROFILE DETERMINES STRATEGY

Ritual profile

Four broad ritual profiles are referred to throughout the guide.

Institutional: People who identify with a religion and regularly practise religious rituals (at least once or twice a month).

Distanced: People who identify with a religion and practise religious rituals occasionally (once a year or less).

Secular: People, often called nones, who identify with secular or humanist values and practise secular rituals.

Alternative: People who identify with holistic or esoteric beliefs and rituals.

Ritual practice

Type of ritual practice (rather than frequency) is the second determining factor for ritual profile.

Traditional: People who feel most at ease with time-honoured customs that are transmitted from generation to generation will choose conventional ceremonial ritual.

Modern: People who value meaningfulness over custom may feel more at ease with an approach that involves innovation and creativity.

Although this guide can serve the needs of people of all profiles, it is most useful for those with *secular* and *alternative* profiles who prefer *modern* ritual practice because little has yet been written to meet their need for ritual.

Arranging obsequies for people with *institutional* profile and *traditional* practice is usually straightforward (see Figure 5.1). Conventional funeral rites best suit this ritual profile. A person with *institutional* identity and *modern* practice may require a personalized religious funeral.

People with a *distanced* profile[10] are by far the most challenged when it comes to arranging a meaningful ceremony. The tools presented here were originally designed for them. Too often their profound need for ritual goes unmet; the risk of them choosing an inappropriate ritual strategy is high. For a person with a *distanced* profile but very *traditional* practice consider a religious ceremony with personalized aspects. For those with a *distanced* and *modern* profile a custom ceremony is usually the most suitable.

A funeral with a celebrant from a traditional humanist group is most likely to fit people with a profile composed of *secular* identity and *traditional* practice. Those with *secular* identity and *modern* practice may choose a ceremony with either a humanist or a non-religious celebrant. The needs of a person with an *alternative* identity and *traditional* or *modern* practice may be met by a ceremony presided by a neo-shaman or a non-religious celebrant.

---

10   Over 20 per cent of the world's population is now religiously unaffiliated. Concretely, this means that there are more than 1.1 billion people with distanced, secular or alternative profiles. Some experts predict that, while the overall number of unaffiliated people around the world will decline to 13 per cent by 2050, the percentage of unaffiliated in much of Europe and North America is expected to increase: in Europe, the percentage could grow from 18 per cent in 2010 to 23 per cent in 2050. In North America it may rise from an estimated 16 per cent of the total population (including children) in 2010 to 26 per cent in 2050 (Pew Research Center 2015).

OUR NEED
FOR RITUAL

Ritualizing is an innate behaviour.
Part II proposes an updated view of ritual along
with a ritual toolbox that contains practical tools
for determining ritual profile, as well as techniques for
dealing with the stress of death, dying and loss.

3

THE SENSE OF RITUAL

Sophia, 92 years old, was killed by a distracted cyclist as she was crossing the street. The Howard family respected their spinster great-aunt's wishes for a simple graveside funeral. Taking up the challenge meant dealing with logistics as well as the many distractions inherent to an outdoor ceremony: uncertain weather conditions, especially wind and rain; having to stand in an awkward configuration between other graves; lack of microphone and sound system; the presence of other mourners and gardeners working on nearby graves; the unsettling sight of the casket and open grave...

The family squeezed in Sophia's small apartment to prepare the ceremony. Harold, the eldest of Sophia's grand-nephews, was appointed to preside. Two nieces and a nephew agreed to write a short homage. Peter, a great-grand-nephew, volunteered to hire and set up a portable sound system for music and a microphone. As the family poked about in Sophia's home they discovered remnants of her life with Beat Generation artists in San Francisco and activism with the LGBT movement alongside thousands of crocheted squares and doilies. Memories flooded back as they tried to sync Sophia's quiet existence with this new perspective on her life.

The day of Sophia's funeral dawned overcast but stiflingly hot. Peter arrived at the gravesite early to set up a few parasols and prepare to greet the family with 'Our Lips Are Sealed' by the Go-Gos. Harold opened the ceremony and read the short homage. Each person paid tribute to Sophia with a short story about her based on an object they'd chosen from her affairs. At the end of the 15-minute long funeral, after the coffin was lowered into the ground, Harold reminded everyone that lunch would be served at his home and closed the ceremony by asking them to take leave of Sophia with a final gesture. As Peter played 'Shooting Star' by Cris Williamson, dozens of crocheted shapes floated down like colourful snowflakes on Sophia's coffin.

Figure 3.1. Ritual power
The Flower Power[1] movement inspired guerrilla theatre, epitomized by the Bread and Puppet Theatre in New York City, handing out balloons and flowers with anti-war literature. In much the same way, ritual power captures imaginations today. Temporary artistic actions that honour the victims of a disaster or an untimely death with flowers, toys, candles and notes are expressions of contemporary ritual power. This photo, taken in Paris in January 2015, shows an ephemeral tribute to the 12 people killed and 11 injured in an attack on the French satirical newspaper *Charlie Hebdo*.

All living creatures experience death. Our curiosity about this inevitable end leads us to explore how others deal with it. By observing mammals, we learn that elephants grieve over fallen family members and chimpanzee mothers may refuse to give up their dead babies. One persistent chimpanzee carried her dead baby around and cared for it for two months (Alpert 2020). By digging up burial sites, we find that human beings have responded to the deaths of those close to them with special

---

[1]   The expression Flower Power was coined by the US Beat poet Allen Ginsberg in 1965 as a means to transform war protests into peaceful affirmative spectacles (Mandeville-Gamble 2007, p.3).

treatment of the bodies throughout history.[2] A grave in Skhul cave at Qafzeh in Israel, thought to be that of a mother and child, contains sea shells, 71 pieces of red ochre and ochre-stained tools[3] that appear to have been prepared and placed with care on or near the corpses (Alpert 2020). These often elaborate and time-consuming activities came to be known as funeral customs or rituals.

WHAT IS RITUAL FOR?

Sensemaking[4] and ritualmaking[5] are clearly not just prehistoric concerns. Think of the permanent war monuments scattered across Europe, and of the ephemeral memorials that pop up at the scene of traffic accidents, disasters, or an attack on innocent civilians (see Figure 3.1).[6] Why expend vital resources in such behaviour? What purpose does ritual serve?

Ritual serves three main functions:

MEET BIOLOGICAL NEEDS

I have long been intrigued by people's profound need to 'do something' to mark a transition in their life. The penny dropped while reading the work of ethnologist Ellen Dissanayake. While observing people go about their everyday lives, Dissanayake noticed that they avidly engage in playful, artistic and ritual pursuits. She became convinced that these activities

---

2   The oldest known intentional burial by humans dates back to about 100,000 years ago.
3   Red ochre is regularly found in Upper Palaeolithic grave sites around the world.
4   Sensemaking is the process by which people make sense of their experiences. The term 'sensemaking', studied by different disciplines under other names for centuries, has marked scientific research since the 1970s. It is widely used today in specific social sciences such as philosophy, sociology, cognitive science and especially social psychology and interdisciplinary research programmes.
5   The term 'ritualmaking' refers to the process by which people create rituals to make sense of their life event experiences. Like the word sensemaking, it is now used by researchers and practitioners alike.
6   In her article 'Commemorative Ritual and the Power of Place' (2017), Irene Stengs addresses the increasing need to commemorate violent deaths (traffic deaths, killings, work-related tragedies) in the public domain.

represent a biologically endowed need. She called this compelling and 'deliberately *nonordinary*' activity 'making special' (1992, pp.42–48).

Need to do something

The death of someone to whom we feel close or even the loss of something precious can throw off our capacity for self- and social regulation.[7] The advice to 'keep busy' addresses our profound need to do something. Performing meaningful rituals in public spaces with others – rather than cleaning the cupboards alone at home – contributes effectively to our emotional and physical wellbeing. Doing something or 'making special' engages our minds, bodies and hearts in concrete activity that promotes healing.

Need to feel safe

Some years ago, during my training in Somatic Experiencing (SE), I discovered an unexpected link between my roles as psychotherapist and celebrant. Psychotherapy, like ritual practice, is effective in settings that meet our profound need to feel safe and connected. Moreover, 'the efficient use of rituals', observes Stephen Porges, 'promotes a physiological state[8] associated with "safety of self" that projects calmness and acceptance towards the other' (2020).

Need to contain strong emotion

Whether we are survivors of trauma or mourners at a funeral, our main concern is to keep from being overwhelmed by the aftereffects of highly charged life experiences. Ritual is a multisensory emotional and communal experience, 'an overlooked asset to the healing of trauma

---

7   Self- and social regulation refers to our ability to calm down (reduce emotional activation) and feel safe in upsetting or novel situations.

8   In a safe environment, says Stephen Porges, when a person no longer needs to be vigilant in anticipation of danger, the nervous system tends to shift into a qualitatively and measurably different physiological 'safe' state. His polyvagal theory (2011) explains the function of this state and how it is supported by the practice of age-old collective and spiritual practices such as communal chanting, various breathing techniques and other such methods that facilitate shifts in the autonomic nervous system (Porges 2020).

and to restoring broken connections' (Levine 2010, p.256; 2017). A funeral ceremony that is well prepared and presided provides a safe container for grief. As our sense of security is enhanced by this external support we can begin to deal with and contain strong overwhelming emotions. In turn, we feel supported, less alone, less afraid and more in control.

This understanding of the adaptive nature of ritual and of how it addresses our sense of security and connectedness changed how I went about ritualmaking.

Dissanayake: Ritual is adaptive

As we now know, hormones released during prolonged stress are debilitating to a wide range of bodily functions, including immune system activity, mental performance, growth and tissue repair, and reproductive physiology and behaviour.

Our ancestors who participated in group rituals were doubtless less stressed than those who, in contrast, went their own isolate, anxious ways. The elaborate messages of ceremonies are meant to attract spirits, ancestors and other forces that affect human lives. By joining with others in music and art-filled rituals, individuals may then – as now – have felt more competent to deal with life's uncertainties and accompanying physical stresses. (Dissanayake 2006, pp.34–5)

MARK TIME AND SPACE

Our ultramodern[9] era has introduced changes that distort our sense of time and space. New uses of energy, for example, make it possible to light up our cities and homes 24/7. Long-distance travel, which used

---

9   French philosopher Frédéric Lenoir prefers the term 'ultramodern' to 'postmodern' because the latter gives the false impression that we are disenchanted with the myth of progress and the modern process when in fact we are in the midst of an unprecedented acceleration of modernity (critical reason, individualization, globalization).

to take years, is now measured in days or hours. The belief that the 'sky is the limit' collapsed with the first step of humankind on the moon. As our traditional vertical reference points (gods, heavens) and horizontal landmarks (borders, bollards) disappear, we are forced to build these safety zones for and within ourselves (Lenoir 2012, p.64).

Trauma and mourning play havoc with our sense of time, space and safety, which, in turn, increases the risk of (re)traumatization. Increasingly, I observe a reduced capacity to construct such safe zones among my clients, especially teens and young adults. The hazards of our ultramodern era contribute to their inability to feel grounded. This in turn affects cognitive, sensory and emotional processes such as memory, perception and attention as well as emotional regulation and prosocial behaviour.

As we saw in Chapter 2, funeral rituals can effectively mark the transition from one phase of loss to the next, inaugurate a new reality within which the bereaved may evolve in peace (Smyth, personal communication 2014). The ceremony, but also time off work, receiving food and messages from well-wishers and sorting through the deceased's affairs, represents a spectrum of funerary rituals, both public and private, that offer survivors specific times and places to mourn. More generally, ritual activity reinforces natural rhythms, especially when it is tied to anniversaries and the passing of the seasons.

ANCHOR MEMORIES

Performing rituals in a safe context modifies our concept of time and how it passes, but also what that passing means. Pliny's account of the eruption of Mount Vesuvius (see Chapter 1), demonstrates how traumatic reactions to helplessness can produce 'an aberration of memory' (Scaer 2001, p.43). Unlike normal memories, which are mutable and dynamically change over time, traumatic memories remain fixed and static. These imprints (engrams) leave deep impressions carved into the sufferer's brain, body and psyche that do not yield easily to change – nor do they readily update with current information (Levine 2015). Whether such memories are consciously accessible or hidden from our everyday awareness, they hinder the ability to live fully in the present and impede adequate preparation for the future, which in turn wreaks havoc on health and social relationships such as marriages, families and friendships (Scaer 2005, p.152; 2012, p.114).

I have often seen intense feelings of helplessness attenuated during a fitting ceremony that introduces new sensory information such as sense of time, place and safety. These upgraded sensations, in particular smell, form rescripted memories and emotions that, when accessed anew, empower rather than overpower. Through ritual practice, the tranquil feelings of aliveness and ecstatic self-transcendence that make us fully human can become enduring features of our existence (Levine 2005, p.xvii).

ATTITUDES TOWARDS RITUAL CHANGE

In early, less hierarchical cultures, hunter-gatherer groups shared ritualmaking or assumed it informally on an ad hoc basis (Smyth, personal communication 2016). With the advent of urbanization, institutions took over ceremonial ritualmaking, which distanced people from this creative process and from the care of the dead. According to historian Patrick J. Geary, our present abandonment of the dead is the end result of a gradual process in Western societies that began in the Middle Ages. As in Roman times, people could – and did – die at any age, with appalling frequency and suddenness. Death came to mark a transition to a new status; it was not experienced as an end. The living maintained ties to their dead loved ones. At the very least, the living had the obligation of *memoria*, remembrance (Geary 1994, p.2). Over the centuries, the disparity between these obligations and funeral practices widened remarkably.

During the Renaissance, Western attitudes towards life, death and the human body began to change (see Figure 3.2).[10] Humanist studies spawned two concepts, secular and ritual, that contributed to greater regard for the arts, scientific discovery and humankind as a species – all of

---

10   See the lyrics of *Passacaglia della vita* in the frontispiece.

which challenged the influence of powerful institutions. Religious leaders and scientific scholars were increasingly pitted against each other. The tensions that persist among scholars and non-scholars alike are due, at least in part, to a misalignment of the concepts secular and ritual as subcategories of religion.[11]

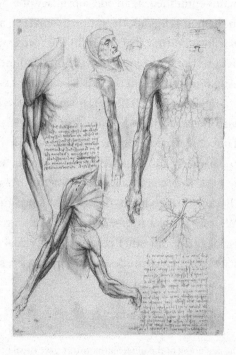

Figure 3.2. Drawing of a dead or moribund man
Renaissance artists like Leonardo da Vinci (1452–1519) became anatomists in order to render more lifelike portrayals of the human figure. See the artist's rendition of the dying man's face (top centre). Body donation remains important today for understanding the human body and for making advancements in science.
© Public Domain. This pen and ink drawing (traces of wash) belongs
to Her Majesty Queen Elizabeth II's Royal Collection

---

11   Atheists, agnostics and humanists live with a negative social profile (non-religious). While it would be absurd to consider non-English languages as a subcategory of English, university departments and publishing houses do just that. The secular, which constitutes a very broad worldview, has long been perceived as a subcategory of another worldview, 'religion'. Adopting a perspective of action that looks at how people 'do' ritual, rather than at the rituals they 'have', offers a logical and comprehensive frame of reference that takes into account the many different worldviews.

Over the last century, ritual experts led us to believe that all ritual is religious, or at least sacred.[12] Conventional definitions describe ritual as irrational, repetitive behaviour that is composed of a series of acts that are circumscribed by tradition or sacerdotal decree and performed according to a prescribed order in religious ceremonies. The secular[13] – which began, and remains enmeshed, as an odd subsidiary of religion – became associated with the non-religious, the rational, science – and ritual void.

The post-war Beat culture that began in the 1950s and became the hippie movement in the mid-1960s evolved into a counterculture that sought to raise up humanity from the gruesomeness of two world wars and the threat of nuclear attack. The movements captured the collective imagination with their accents on peace, love and social engagement. People stepped out of routine comfort zones to explore new opportunities for expressing, separately and together, what it means to be human in our world. The period served as a sandbox for the arts and the art of ritualmaking. Early efforts to break free from the institutional rigidity of traditional Western ritual were characterized by a search for meaning through the use of rites from other cultures[14] and ritual improvisation and spontaneity.[15] The new attitudes had an impact on scholars in the

---

12   Thinkers at the beginning of the nineteenth century gave ritual broad and inclusive definitions that intrinsically tied it to religion. Asad notes that, when decoding ritual symbols, anthropologists 'incorporated theological preoccupations into an avowedly secular intellectual task' (1993, pp.55–60). Like Douglas, he sees the secular as neither continuous with the religious (phase) that supposedly preceded it, nor a simple break from it (Asad 2003, p.24).

13   Scholars like anthropologist Mary Douglas hold that religion and secularism are two types of worldview. Secularism is 'an age-old cosmological type, a product of a definable social experience, which need have nothing to do with urban life or modern science...[or] transcendent explanations and powers', which can turn up in any historical age and locale (Douglas, cited in Bell 2009 [1997], p.200).

14   Alan Watts: 'When somebody comes in from the Orient with a new religion which hasn't got any [horrible] associations in our minds, all the words are new, all the rites are new, and yet, somehow it has feeling in it, and we can get with that, you see, and we can dig that!' (quoted in Cohen 1991, n.p.).

15   Both 'beatniks' and hippies invented ritual performances where 'improvisation, direct experience, immediacy, and spontaneity were priorities' (Aukeman 2016, p.107).

arts and spawned ritual studies, which acknowledged the ties between theory and practice.[16]

Some decades on, the word 'ritual' escaped the scholarly realm to appear everywhere. Google 'ritual' to see how it punctuates mundane discussions on sleep and dental hygiene, pops up on Internet forums about pet and plant care and is even embossed on classy hockey sticks, designer coffee labels and cosmetics. In the end, it was not Darwin that pinched ritual from religious institutions but the marketing industry. Marketing experts give ritual a savvy makeover that untethers it from religion – while still surfing on its transcendent wave – paving the way for consumerism,[17] yet another major paradigm shift.[18]

Like any marketing message, the buzz created around ritual can be positive or negative. On the upside, the emphasis on connection grounds society in its earthy *Homo sapiens* roots, serving as a counterpoise to virtuality, loneliness and a wrenching sense of social dislocation. On the downside, people who find traditional rituals meaningless rarely find consumer ritual a satisfying substitute.

Some domains, apparently impervious to these different popular metamorphoses of ritual, persist in welding it to religious belief and the supernatural.[19] Ritual appears in many eras, cultures, environments and contexts but it is not the same thing everywhere – how do we explain that? Clearly, our ideas of ritual need a serious update.

---

16 Catherine Bell, in particular, recognized the dangers of a philosophical split between thought and action, observer and observed. She brought clarity to ritual studies with her profound insight that 'ritual, long thought of as thoughtless action stripped of context, is more interestingly understood as a culturally strategic way of acting in the world. Ritual is a form of social activity' (Jonte-Pace 2009, p.vii).

17 Consumerism, like secularism and religion, is a worldview.

18 Scientist Thomas Kuhn popularized the concept of 'paradigm shift' nearly 60 years ago, arguing that scientific advancement is not evolutionary, but a 'series of peaceful interludes punctuated by intellectually violent revolutions,' during which 'one conceptual worldview is replaced by another' (1996 [1962], p.10).

19 Archaeologist Richard Bradley deplores the fact that the dead are still discussed in a language that is dying, thus excluding important findings from research. He exposes how a narrow view of ritual affects archaeological practice: a small selection of artefacts that men used, like axes, may be identified as special and ritually charged but others, such as the quernstones used by women for cooking, are treated as refuse and casually discarded (Bradley 2003, p.5).

UPDATING OUR IDEAS OF RITUAL

Perceiving ritual as a culturally strategic form of social activity helps shift our focus towards how people from different cultures and times 'do' ritual and away from the rituals people 'have'. What becomes obvious from this perspective is that ritual is, and has always been, culturally constructed. Variation in what, when, where, how and how frequently rituals are crafted and practised is the norm, not ritual uniformity.

The same goes for language. All peoples everywhere communicate using culturally constructed languages that have different structures, music, rhythms and words. The fact that there are no satisfactory English equivalents for words like *vordenker* (German), *saudades* (Portuguese), *gezellig* (Dutch), *komorebi* (Japanese) or *flâner* (French) may prove frustrating for translators, but it does not question whether or not English is a language.

Taking the analogy a bit further, ritual and language are both composed of verbal and non-verbal aspects: words, acts, gestures and body expressions. A baby first communicates with others using the rudiments of both language (sounds) and ritual (facial gestures). Both behaviours are learned and evolve over time. They vary tremendously from one era, culture, geographical environment and social context to the next.

RITUAL ACCULTURATION

Individuals from different cultures construct rituals differently out of different information. Changes in spatial, temporal, environmental and even climatic conditions affect how rituals are made, evolve and practised. The rituals of people who move to another culture or subculture adapt to the affective and social logic of the new context. This is the case of the nones mentioned earlier; they acculturate to a new context or era less influenced by religion. Young people who go to university usually show signs of ritual acculturation. The same goes for immigrants exposed to the rituals of a new culture. Ritual practice evolves rapidly for people who move from rural to urban contexts. The same thing happens from one generation to another.

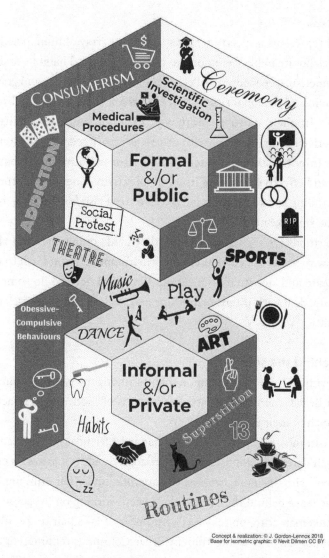

Concept & realization: © J. Gordon-Lennox 2018
Base for isometric graphic: © Nevit Dilmen CC BY

Figure 3.3. Spectrum of ritual activity

This figure illustrates two main spheres of ritual activity: formal/public and informal/
private. The arts, situated in the middle, represent resources for ritual expression in
both spheres. The hexagonal isometric representation is nearly an infinity symbol;
relatively few rigid lines divide the different formal and informal activities. Moreover,
formal ritual activity is often mirrored in the informal sphere. Ceremonies considered
unacceptable to the status quo, for example, are often referred to as superstition.
Consumerism and addiction are mirrored in the private sphere with obsessive
compulsive behaviours.

RITUAL, A SPECTRUM OF HUMAN ACTIVITY

Ritual represents a spectrum that spans a vast array of human activities, from elaborate public ceremony to intimate personal habits – and even consumerism (see Figure 3.3). People commonly experience and gravitate to public and personal rituals that help them to be a good and typical person in their culture. Moreover, experiencing these culturally normative rituals, alone or with others, is associated with greater well-being. **Intentionality is a determining factor in doing ritual that feels right and effective.** In and of itself, ritual activity is neutral: it promotes love, healing and social cohesion (#MeToo) but also foments war, hatred and racism (fake news).

As rituals are regularly updated, they guide individuals and groups on how to act in the current era and environment. From birth to death, we create and 'do ritual' to meet our biological need to do something, feel safe, deal with intense emotions and anchor our memories firmly in reality.

Behind the scenes...

Death and loss were common themes among the vibrant community of Beat Generation artists. Expressions of mourning characterize much of their work.

In 1965, when Jay DeFeo and her artist friends were evicted from their derelict building in San Francisco, Jay could not just walk out the door with *The Rose*, her two-ton artwork, under her arm; nor could she leave behind the project she'd been working on for seven years (Aukeman 2016, pp.145–6). The transfer of Jay's painting-sculpture, immortalized in a short film by Bruce Connor, is reminiscent of the ritual removal of a corpse by a first call coach to lie in state. The walls around DeFeo's workroom are demolished so that a forklift can shift the crated piece out of the building and load it on a removal van. Bereft, Jay contemplates the defenestration from a fire escape, her legs dangling over the void. In the aftermath of the removal, DeFeo retreated for almost three years, 'to rest and retrieve her sense of self, separate from *The Rose*' (Green and Levy 2003, p.3). Eventually, her monumental oeuvre found a final resting place at the Whitney Museum in New York.

Beat Generation icon Allen Ginsberg gave direction to his own funeral saying that he did not really care what his friends and family did with his body or ashes. But he did want a big funeral (see his poem 'Death and Fame', 1997). True to his unique generous style, Ginsberg left his personal and financial affairs in order. Before he died, he also called nearly everyone in his address book to say goodbye (Morgan 2007, p.649). As per his last wishes, after a more or less private wake where Buddhist texts and Kaddish were chanted, Ginsberg had his big funeral. In fact, he had several: Ginsberg's friends divided up his cremains and ceremonially placed them in three places he loved. His fans organized several memorial services around the world.

NOTES ON REPACKAGING RITUAL

French poet Stéphane Mallarmé (1842–1898) allegedly said: 'To define is to kill. To suggest is to create.' Definitions of ritual proliferate; most refer to dated concepts of ceremonial ritual.[20] Adding yet another definition to the pack does not make sense. Instead, the guidelines below stimulate creativity by juxtaposing what ritual is and is not.

VOLUNTARY, NOT IMPOSED

Mourners should pay particular attention to their own body sensations; it is natural to feel numb at first. Feeling safe in one's own body and sensing the support of one's entourage are essential to the grieving process. Although the chief mourners need to be actively involved in a custom ceremony, both adults

---

20 Ronald L. Grimes presents several pages of erudite definitions of ritual in the Appendices to his book *The Craft of Ritual Studies* (2014).

and children should be able to choose, without regret, how they participate. Children and teens are particularly vulnerable in the face of death. Young children rarely have enough experience of death to know what it implies. They may not dare refuse suggestions made by an adult caretaker. If they seem reticent or openly refuse to see the body or do not want to attend the funeral, their wish should be respected. Never leave a child alone with a dead body.

AUTHENTICITY, NOT PARODY

'I am the only one who can tell the story of my life and say what it means' says Dorothy Allison (1996, p.70). Our relationship with the deceased must be recounted in our own words, using objects and symbols that remind us of her or him. These are the building blocks of authentic funeral rituals.

Culture has always been enriched by the exchange of ideas. Nonetheless, borrowing rituals that use objects, words and gestures from other people's traditions rarely makes sense and can be seen as disrespectful. Some of my colleagues are regularly solicited for indigenous rituals. Not long ago, traditional leaders of several Native American tribes declared war on those who usurp the ritual elements of their spiritual tradition (People's Path 1993). Our fundamental need to mark a death does not justify borrowing, or stealing, rituals from other people's cultures. Rituals studies expert Ronald L. Grimes warns against grafting elements we do not understand into our ceremonies because of the strong risk that we end up with something that we cannot fully absorb (Grimes, personal communication 2016).

PLAYFUL, NOT A GAME

Bespoke ritual is not child's play; it cannot be improvised. Much like a fun clever game, ritual requires significant behind-the-scenes design. Nearly every funeral is composed of a few playful stories and light-hearted memories but a funeral is not a game, it is for real.

ARTISTIC, NOT ART

Art is a resource for ritualmaking, not an end in itself.[21] Ritual-making does not require that the results be skilful, or even beautiful. When integrating ordinary objects, places, sounds and actions into a ceremony we deliberately make them extraordinary. A simple flower arrangement, a book, a wooden cooking spoon become something special when they are used to speak of relationships with the dead. Tables and chairs set out in a pleasing way may reveal the deceased's aesthetic tastes, and the bereaved's concern for the comfort of those who mourn with them.

THERAPEUTIC, NOT THERAPY

Whether the funeral is for a person who had a long life, a mother of young children, a father who died by suicide or a child who was terminally ill, the presider, much like a psychotherapist, must be able to provide a safe setting for emotionally charged sentiments. Although support for strong emotion during the ceremony may well be therapeutic, therapy is not the end purpose of ritual. The reason why we use ritual should not be confused with its possible benefits. While the desired outcomes may be similar, intention and process are quite different. Psychotherapy is about treatment of dis-ease: mitigating troublesome behaviours, beliefs, compulsions, thoughts or emotions. Ritual is not a direct or efficient treatment for these ills.

---

21 'Art for art's sake' or 'l'art pour l'art', a slogan credited to Théophile Gautier (1811–1872), was a reaction among Western artists against the idea that art had to serve some practical, moral or didactic purpose. It presents art as an independent and well-defined domain in itself that is solely concerned with aesthetics, imagination, enjoyment and the self-expression of the artist. George Sand and Friedrich Nietzsche criticized the slogan, claiming that art 'for art's sake' just does not exist. Postcolonial African writers such as Léopold Senghor and Chinua Achebe consider the phrase a Eurocentric view on art and creation.

TIME-OUT-OF-TIME, NOT TIME-OUT

When a funeral feels right there is often a salutary time-out-of-time sensation[22] where feelings are richer and more intense than usual. Chief mourners, together with the assembly, slip from ordinary to extraordinary time. This heightened experience, which is at once individual and collective, occurs only in settings that are perceived as safe. People feel present and are aware that whatever is happening – be it happy or sad – will sooner or later come to an end. As the ceremony draws to a close, they may notice saliva in their mouth and moisture in their eyes, take a deep breath, sigh, stretch, smile or yawn. There is a sense of release or relief. The brain's timekeeper[23] adjusts and returns to normal time. This phenomena is commonly experience during both traditional and emerging ritual that feels right.

In the case of a ceremony that feels wrong, the opposite occurs, with physical signs of high stress: the eyes and mouth feel dry, muscles are tense, posture is stiff and breathing may be shallow or irregular. The brain's timekeeper goes offline and mourners are left with a time-out sensation that is highly unpleasant and destabilizing.

THEATRICAL, NOT THEATRE

The funeral is theatrical in that, like a play, it should be based on a clear script. When I train professional celebrants, I invite an actor to work with us on the use of space, voice, diction and scenography. The assembly's sense of safety is enhanced when the ceremony flows smoothly and yields no surprises or improvised contributions. This requires advance preparation

---

22   Time-out-of-time refers to the salutary experience of self- and social regulation that occurs during funeral rituals that feel right. Time-out describes the opposite process which induces a sense of disorientation or dysfunction, which can lead to alienation, isolation and even fear. Time-out-of-time differs from Mihaly Csikszentmihalyi's concept of 'flow' or even 'group flow' in that it occurs among a diversified assembly that has no express or implied objectives.

23   The scientific name for the timekeeper is the dorsolateral prefrontal cortex (DLPFC). It is responsible for 'telling us how our present experience relates to the past and how it may affect the future' (van der Kolk 2014, p.69).

that includes plotting out, in choreographic sequences, the movements of the participants. If a microphone is required, have each speaker test it in advance. A funeral is theatrical but it is not theatre. Meaningful ritual is based on genuine intention and performance.

CELEBRATION, NOT A PARTY

A funeral ceremony, like the one Kerry's friends organized, was festive but it was hardly a party. It was a bittersweet occasion described by those present as more bitter than sweet. Yet the bitterness of loss was sweetened by the presence of well-meaning people, words of sympathy and kind touch at the informal social gathering that followed. Sometimes referred to as a reception or a wake, this second part of the funeral is in fact an extension of the ceremony itself. Ideally, the social interaction transforms into mutual support and long-term commitment to keeping memories alive.

WASTE NOT, WANT NOT

Although few organizers even think of working towards zero waste, most funerals typically produce significant quantities of rubbish and waste material. 'How many funerals are we going to have?!' 'So what if our carbon imprint[24] is high, just this once.' 'Launching balloons would make the funeral so much less sad.' 'Who wants to wash dishes after everyone leaves?' You don't need to be a tree-hugging environmentalist to reduce waste. It makes sense not only for the planet, but also for us all. Take up the challenge by concentrating on just one area where you will effectively reduce waste. Use your imagination and creativity. You may well find that there are more advantages than disadvantages to your choices.

---

24   What is a 'carbon imprint'? Sometimes referred to as a 'carbon footprint', it is a measure of how much more CO_2 a person uses than is replaced by natural processes or personal environmental action. A multi-language website, www.myclimate.org, calculates the carbon imprint for different activities and modes of transport.

Travel

Reduce the distance your guests will need to travel in motor vehicles. Choose a venue for the funeral ceremony that is close to the cemetery and the reception. One family hired a bus to take their out-of-town guests from the place where the ceremony was held to the cemetery and then to the reception venue. If you decide to do so, let people know about this option beforehand. Put it in the death announcement and have the presider remind people again at the beginning and at the end of the ceremony.

Tableware

Consider the impact of plastic decorations, plates and cutlery. Suitable solutions exist now, such as compostable, recyclable, biodegradable tableware and party decorations that are less toxic for the environment.

Decorations

Choose flowers that are locally grown or that can be planted in a garden (yours or someone else's) or on the gravesite at the cemetery. If advised in advance, the cemetery staff may do this for you at the time of the burial.

Balloons are cheerful and evoke happy memories for most people. Two types of balloons are widely in use: latex and Mylar. Mylar nylon balloons are often coated with a metallic finish; they are not classified as biodegradable and do not decompose. Latex (natural rubber) takes about six months to decompose. Fish, fowl and other animals may die if they ingest bits or get caught in the strings tied to balloons. Neither kind of balloon (Mylar/latex) should be filled with helium and launched on account of the risks to the environment. As an alternative provide latex balloons that are blown up the old-fashioned way, used in a controlled setting and then composted.

Craft things – like origami – from old newspapers and magazine pages. One family cut out hundreds of coloured paper hearts, put them in baskets and had them distributed to people as they arrived at the cemetery for the committal. The sight of handfuls of hearts fluttering down on the casket helped family and friends take leave of their loved one.

4

PREPLANNING MAKES SENSE

*On the morning of 1 November Michael looks out of his window to see two
people driving off in a hearse. He rings his neighbour's bell. The nurse who
opens the door confirms that Mr Brown passed away during the night. She
invites him in for coffee with Maria, Mr Brown's daughter. 'My father would
have been 95 years old next week. As you know, he fell ill about six weeks ago
and insisted on palliative care at home so he could enjoy his flowers to the end...
His garden was his pride and joy, you know. We'll miss him so.'*

*'Yes, we will. He had a long but hard life and was prepared to go... I always
enjoyed Oliver's stories and admired his work,' reminisced Michael. 'Do you
have plans for the funeral?'*

*'Did you know that he'd arranged in advance for a non-religious funeral?
Lisa will preside. He survived all of his close friends. He wanted you to say a
few words. Would you be willing to speak?' asked Maria.*

'Of course,' replied Michael. 'I'd be honoured.'

Obituary notice

*BROWN, Oliver, master shoemaker and artist, aged 94, passed away
peacefully at home, on 31 October. A dedicated husband and father, he is
survived by one daughter, three grandchildren, two great-grandchildren,
a nephew and two great nieces. A funeral service will be held at Peaceful
Repose Crematorium at 11 am on Saturday 6 November. All are welcome
to attend. No flowers, please. Donations, if desired, to the Foundation for
Artisan Shoemakers.*

*The day of the funeral is blustery and cold but bright. In accordance with
Mr Brown's wishes, one of his grandsons, a professional violinist, plays*

a quiet piece as the small assembly gathers. Lisa opens the ceremony by introducing herself and welcoming everyone in the name of Mr Brown's family. Before reading the homage Oliver had prepared with Maria and two great-grandchildren, she draws their attention to an arrangement composed of Mr Brown's gardening tools and beautiful bouquets of flowers from his garden. After another violin piece, Maria, her son, granddaughter and Michael come forward to speak about their relationship with Oliver. Lisa closes the ceremony saying, 'We do not know what happens to us after death. Mr Brown was a matter-of-fact man who was not afraid to die but regretted the separation with his loved ones. He knew it would sadden them.' Lisa invites the assembly to take a few flowers with them before joining the cortege to the columbarium for the final separation. The assembly exits to 'Passacaglia della vita' interpreted by l'Arpeggiata.

Lisa nods to Maria. She steps forward, pulls on a gardening glove and explains that her father had requested cremation so that his ashes nourish the earth. A funeral attendant opens the urn. Maria takes a handful of ashes, pauses, then sprinkles them in the designated area along with flowers from Mr Brown's garden. Family and friends follow suit, choosing to perform the gesture either with ashes and flowers or just with flowers. Lisa closes the funeral with an invitation from the family to join them at a place nearby for stories and light refreshments.

HOW TO PREPLAN A FUNERAL

Advance planning for weddings and vacations is commonplace. Yet few people plan for something that is even more certain to happen: their funeral. The most obvious advantage of preplanning this life event is reducing the burden on those close to you. The second is ensuring your funeral reflects your ritual profile and follows your wishes for ritual strategy. Taking time, now, to arrange your funeral is one less thing your loved ones will have to puzzle over once you've passed.

Preplanning my funeral makes sense, you may say, but how does one go about it? It is not all that difficult if you have a few good tools.

'People need new tools to work with rather than tools that work for them,' exclaimed philosopher Ivan Illich (1973, p.10). He was convinced that people's natural ability to participate in the events and processes that shape their lives enables them to live a more meaningful existence. He argued for convivial tools that meet people's need to take control and allow them to make things in a personalized way that is aligned with their interests and abilities. Convivial also implies companionship. Our natural ability for ritualmaking is facilitated by having a few convivial tools that keep us in tune with ourselves and others.

The toolbox for preplanning[1] a funeral holds the essential tools for preparing ourselves and our loved ones for what lies ahead. It is followed by seven destressing techniques. Part III proposes three more toolboxes, one for each phase of the crafting process – planning, creating and realizing.

Behind the scenes...

Pliny the Younger, a great promoter of preplanning, informed his friend Nonius Maximus of the dangers of avoiding it or of doing so in an untimely manner.

> I am deeply afflicted with the news I have received of the death of Fannius; in the first place, because I loved one so eloquent and refined, in the next, because I was accustomed to be guided by his judgment... He left a will written up quite some time before his death. As a result, his estate has now gone to people who greatly displeased him and his favourites are excluded. (1900, *Letters* LI)

---

1   Although 'preplan' looks like a buzz word from twentieth-century business jargon, it appears as early as 1829 in the writings of Robert Southey, who was poet laureate of England from 1813 to 1843.

TOOLBOX

RITUAL PROFILE

Questionnaire on my ritual profile

Notes on ritual profile and strategy are in Chapter 2. The *Key to the questionnaire on my ritual profile* is located in Chapter 5.

This questionnaire is designed to help you define your own ritual profile and determine the best strategy for ritualizing different life events, from birthdays to weddings to funerals.

Part I Circle the icons next to the statements that best describe you and bar those that do not apply.

- ★ I am an active member of a religious institution.
- ● I am an inactive member of a religious institution.
- ■ I am a member of an organization with humanist or philosophical views.
- ◆ I am attracted to groups that value holistic or esoteric practices.
- ★ I attend religious worship services at least once a month.
- ■ I live by my own ethic which is based on reason and humanistic values.
- ● I attend religious worship services about once or twice a year.
- ◆ Life is a natural process. My life event ceremony should celebrate the mystery, joy and uncertainty of life.
- ■ My wedding/funeral/child's life event ceremony could take place almost anywhere, except in a religious setting.
- ◆ I celebrate nature, am sensitive to the colours of the seasons and marvel at the cosmos.
- ★ I imagine my wedding/funeral/child's ceremony in a religious setting.
- ● I would love to have my wedding/funeral/child's life event ceremony in a religious setting but, if possible, without a priest/pastor/rabbi/imam or other religious leader.
- ■ As human beings, we alone are responsible for solving the environmental problems we have created. No belief in a god or a supernatural force can help us.
- ◆ It is important for me to have a simple funeral and to be buried or have my ashes spread in a natural setting, far from artificial structures.

★   I cannot imagine my wedding/funeral/child's ceremony without a priest/pastor/rabbi/imam or other religious leader.

●   My wedding/child's life event ceremony may be held in a secular setting but I cannot imagine my funeral without religious rites.

◆   A life event ceremony with a shaman would suit me quite well.

●   My family and friends would be disappointed if I did not organize a religious ceremony for my wedding/funeral/child's life event ceremony.

■   I do not need god or any supernatural being in order to live and die well.

★   It is important to have sacred texts and religious rites performed at my wedding/my funeral/our children's life event ceremonies.

■   I want my wedding/funeral/child's ceremony to be presided by a humanist celebrant or at least someone who shares my humanist values.

Part II Circle the icons next to the statements that best describe you and bar those that do not apply.

❖   Religious holidays are important to me because they preserve my cultural and social traditions.

▲   I advocate progressive values and ideals regarding gender and social roles.

❖   Official documents (religious or civil) confirming my wedding/funeral/child's life events are important to me.

▲   A ceremony that celebrates my wedding/funeral/child's life events must correspond to our values rather than to official social or civil standards.

▲   I belong to one or several groups composed of people who come together around projects, leisure activities or ideals.

❖   I am most comfortable with time-tested values, roles and rituals.

▲   I like the idea of having a close friend or non-official person preside over a life event ceremony, such as my wedding, funeral or a naming ceremony for my child.

❖   Only a spiritual or civil leader can validate the ceremony of a life event, such as our wedding, a funeral or a ceremony for our child.

▲   I can imagine holding my wedding/funeral/child's ceremony in a unique setting such as a museum, garden, restaurant, library or on a farm.

Part III Please note below the number of times you have ticked each of these six symbols and, if you wish, your observations.

Observations

★ _____

● _____

■ _____

◆ _____

▲ _____

✣ _____

 Coronach will

This tool is about how to convey your wishes for your funeral to your nearest and dearest.[2] Why should you plan your funeral in advance?

- *You know what you do not want.* After the last funeral you attended you said: 'That is definitely not for me!'
- *You want to foster life and love* (rather than squabbling) among those you care about the most.
- *You are a responsible adult.* Help those close to you channel the energy generated by feelings of grief into creative activity.
- *You want those you love to feel free to think and act outside the box.* Having your ideas, instructions and blessing to craft a funeral event that would have pleased you can bring your nearest and dearest untold pleasure and satisfaction.
- *You want your say in what they spend on your goodbye party.*[3] Even better, leave them the funds to make it happen! The pain of loss

---

2   Obtain permission in advance from the person you name to carry out your wishes.
3   If you appreciate a humorous approach to planning your funeral check out Kyle Tevlin's website (see *Resources: Funerals*).

can be transformed as people come together in an authentic, and cathartic, outcry of the heart.

Will you put down a few simple lines, now, to show that you care about how your loved ones experience those first weeks after your death? It's up to you.

Purpose of my coronach will

Although it is unlikely anyone will be annoyed or upset by this approach, begin by explaining in your own words why you prepared this document. 'Dear *Name*, I'm leaving you these elements and guidelines for my funeral... [see reasons above for inspiration].'

How I view my life

In a sentence or two let them know how *you* view your life and how you want to be remembered. Frank Sinatra allegedly said: 'I would like to be remembered as a man who had a wonderful time living life, a man who had good friends, fine family – and I don't think I could ask for anything more than that, actually.' A woman who felt her friends pitied her for having bad luck in love and health wrote: 'You may do what you wish but respect the following guidelines: No religious ceremony. As far as I am concerned, my life has been good. Please hold a reception at [name of restaurant]. Toast me with [name of her favourite wine]. Use the money in this envelope to cover costs.'

Kind of funeral I do not want

A short list should suffice.

What I enjoy and why

- *What do you find pleasing?* Note information that could be useful for planning your funeral event: places you enjoy; preferred hour of the day or night; favourite foods and drinks; your favourite colours, textures, shapes, films, books, music, sounds, objects... Now, tell us why you like that particular piece of music, food, et cetera.

- *Storytelling*: Reveal the true reason you've kept that stuffed panda bear all these years. Draw up a comic with an funny anecdote. Recall a meaningful experience.
- *Highlights*: What special ties (family or close friendships) or which favourite memories are important to you?

Kind of funeral I do want

How do you imagine your funeral? Are your ideas consistent with your ritual profile (see *Questionnaire on my ritual profile*)? Throwing a funeral party is great. Don't forget to begin with a ceremonial moment. At the very least, a presider should (1) welcome your guests, (2) speak your name, (3) give your date and place of birth and the date and place of your death and (4) explain the intention behind the event. The tools in Part III may help you complete this section.

Brief biography

Make a short list that puts significant events and relationships in chronological or thematic order:

- place and date of birth, full name (also name at birth or before marriage, if applicable; parents' names)
- childhood: family home(s), childhood friends and memories
- education/vocational training: schools, internships, graduation, diplomas
- family life: parents, siblings, godmother, godfather, marriage(s), children, grandchildren...
- experience: professional, volunteer
- interests: sports, hobbies, entertainment, reading, travel, art, languages, spirituality, knowledge of specialized fields, philosophy of life.

List of people to notify

Establish a list of special people you want to be advised of your death and invited to the funeral. Include full names and up-to-date contact information (telephone and email).

Who should craft the ceremony?

Appoint 1-2 people to oversee the creation of the funeral ceremony and the organization of a reception. Encourage them to work in teams and delegate responsibilities.

Ceremony and reception

Where would you like the funeral held? Which setting seems most consistent with your values and what you appreciate in life? Who would you like to participate?

Final resting place

Where do you want your body buried or your ashes spread or interred? Do you have a designated cemetery plot? If so, note the exact address and the name of the contact person. If you want your ashes spread, make sure this is allowed in the place you have chosen.

Obituary notice (optional)

Ensure that your funeral is not used as an opportunity to settle scores by suggesting a draft version. Your family tree is what it is; using your death announcement to prune it is an inelegant move for which others must assume the consequences. Big families may group relatives, for example: '...is survived by... as well as the Smith, Williams and Brown families.'

Inventory on ritual profile for funerals

The questionnaire is designed to help you determine your own ritual strategy. The inventory is useful in determining ritual profile and strategy in the case of a funeral for a loved one. *Notes on ritual profile and strategy* are in Chapter 2. The *Key to the inventory on ritual profile for funerals* is located in Chapter 5.

How well did you know your family member or friend and the kind of funeral she or he would have wanted? Once you are relatively clear about her or his ritual profile it will be easier to determine the best strategy for creating funeral rituals to honour her or his life.

Part 1 Circle the icon next to the statements that best fit your family member or friend and bar those that do not apply.

★ S/he was an active member of a religious institution.

● S/he was an inactive member of a religious institution.

■ S/he was a member of an organization with humanist or philosophical views.

◆ S/he was attracted to groups that value holistic or esoteric practices.

★ S/he attended religious worship services at least once a month.

■ S/he lived by her/his own ethical code that was based on reason and humanistic values.

● S/he attended religious worship services about once or twice a year.

◆ S/he believed in some sort of rebirth (reincarnation, metempsychosis or transmigration) and/or had other esoteric ideas about life and death.

■ S/he would have chosen to have her/his funeral almost anywhere, except in a religious setting.

◆ S/he celebrated nature, was sensitive to the colours of the seasons and marvelled at the cosmos.

★ S/he would want her/his funeral held in a religious setting with a religious leader.

● S/he would have wanted her/his funeral ceremony in a religious setting but, if possible, without a priest/pastor/rabbi/imam or other religious leader.

■ In her/his view, Epicurus got it right: 'When death is there, we are not; when we are there, death is not.'

◆ S/he would have wanted a simple funeral reception in a natural setting, far from artificial structures.

★ S/he was comforted knowing s/he would go to heaven and see her/his lost loved ones when s/he died.

● S/he was not religious, but s/he was practical. S/he would not have objected to having the funeral in a religious setting or at a funeral parlour simply because it would be easier to organize.

◆ A funeral ceremony presided by a shaman would have suited her/him quite well.

● It comforted her/him to know that s/he would not disappear when s/he died.

■   In her/his view, no god or any supernatural beings are necessary for living and dying well.

★   S/he would have wanted sacred texts read and religious rites performed at her/his funeral.

■   S/he would have wanted her/his ceremony to be performed by a humanist celebrant or at least someone who shares her/his humanist values.

Part II Circle the icons next to the statements that best describe your family member or friend and bar those that do not apply.

❖   Religious holidays were important to her/him because they preserved her/his cultural and social traditions.

▲   S/he advocated progressive values and ideals regarding gender and social roles.

❖   Official documents (religious or civil) confirming her/his wedding/funeral/child's life events were important to her/him.

▲   A ceremony celebrating her/his wedding/funeral/child's life events would have to correspond to her/his values rather than to official social or civil standards.

▲   S/he belonged to one, or several groups composed of people who come together around projects, leisure activities or ideals.

❖   S/he was most comfortable with time-tested values, roles and rituals.

▲   S/he liked the idea of having a close friend or non-official person preside over a life event ceremony, such as her/his wedding, funeral or a naming ceremony for her/his child.

❖   Only a spiritual or civil leader could validate the ceremony of a life event, such as a wedding, a funeral or a ceremony for her/his child.

▲   S/he could have imagined holding her/his wedding/funeral/child's ceremony in a unique setting such as a museum, garden, restaurant, library or on a farm.

Part III Please note below the number of times you have ticked each of these six symbols and, if you wish, your observations.

Observations

★ _____

● _____

■ _____

◆ _____

▲ _____

✤ _____

SEVEN DESTRESSING TECHNIQUES

As I waited with mourners for a funeral to begin, the son of the deceased mentioned that their family doctor had given them 'something to help them get through it'.[4] Regrettably, the emotional cushion offered by such drugs can have negative short- and long-term implications for the grief process. Anaesthetized mourners are unlikely to fully benefit from the support they receive. They remain sad, lonely and disconnected after the service and feel alone in the weeks, months and years that follow the funeral.

Grief is neither a physical nor a mental illness. How we deal with it can influence how we remember the funeral and our loved one.

---

4   Pharmaceuticals should be used with extreme caution. Powerful benzodiazepine drugs are often prescribed to treat anxiety and panic disorders. Negative effects may include trouble with cognitive skills, memory and concentration, slurred speech, changes in sex drive and mood, drowsiness and headache. At high doses people may experience respiratory problems, confusion, disorientation and coma. Overdose becomes increasingly likely if the drugs are used in conjunction with other depressant substances, including alcohol.

Neurobiological advances open doors on body-based methods for dealing with mourning in a multisensory manner.

The seven destressing techniques described below represent corporeal technology that requires no particular conditions or skill. They can be used almost anywhere and any time by nearly everyone. Even a child can do 'Near and far' as he waits for the ceremony to begin. Use these techniques before and during any high stress events. Unlike mind-numbing drugs, these mind-body-viscera-based remedies and exercises make use of our senses, breath, attention shifts and movement to keep us fully present and in tune with our basic needs and desires.

Remedies (Smell and touch)

Destressing remedies calm the nervous system through smell and touch. Ironically, bitter orange trees yield three oils that can help smoothen the emotional ups and downs of grief. Neroli (*Citrus aurantium*) is an essential oil produced from the blossom of the tree. Massage a drop onto a wrist or the base of the neck before the funeral to help alleviate anxiety and heart palpitations. Petitgrain oil (*Citrus bigardia*) has a woodier aroma because it is derived from the tree's leaves and young twigs. This oil has a good reputation as a nerve tonic and can help with nervous exhaustion as well as stress-related anger and panic. Bergamot oil (*Citrus bergamia*) comes from the peel of the bergamot orange (another kind of orange tree). It can help with depression, stress, tension, fear, hysteria, anorexia, eczema and general convalescence.

In aromatherapy all three oils are known for their calming and relaxing scent. One drop of essential oil suffices. Mix two drops with massage oil and apply to the feet or stomach area to relax and lessen stress. Better yet, ask a friend to massage it on your back. Applied in the same way lavender (*Lavandula angustifolia*), lemongrass (*Cymbopogon citratus*) and lemon balm (*Melissa officinalis*) combat stress, anxiety and sleeplessness.

Hugging (Using touch with others)

Do this exercise with a partner. The exercise can calm activation and relieve anxiety and feelings of fear. It is suitable for children and adults. Where there is a great difference in size, such as with small children, the person needing soothing can be held. This exercise is not appropriate in the face of real threat. When activation is called for the exercise is counterproductive. Never practise it with a person with whom you do not feel very comfortable on a physical level.

- *Positioning*: Stand face to face with your partner with your feet shoulder-width apart and flat on the floor (barefoot or stocking foot is recommended). Place your arms around each other, lean into each other lightly. Focus on yourself. Feel your insides quieting down. Let the hug last until you feel still inside (30 seconds to 3 minutes). An alternative version involves touching foreheads, with or without placing your hands on the other person's shoulders. This version is recommended in contexts where full-length body contact is unacceptable. Rocking has a similar effect and can be done alone (e.g. the rocking in traditional Jewish prayer).
- *For clinicians*: This exercise effectively calms activation. One psychotherapist advises its use to enhance one's physical and emotional relationship with a partner (Schnarch 1997, pp.157–186).

 Butterfly hug (Using touch alone)

The butterfly hug is a self-soothing technique practised alone. It is suitable for anyone who can follow the simple instructions.

- *Positioning*: Turn the palms of your hands towards you and cross your wrists. Interlock your thumbs to form the butterfly's body. Your hands and other fingers are the butterfly wings. Place your thumbs against your upper chest, just below the intersection of the clavicles. (*Alternative position*: Cross your arms high over your chest and place the tips of your middle fingers lightly on your shoulders, thumbs pointing towards your throat.) Your eyes may be closed, partially closed or even open if you feel safer this way. Turn your eyes inwards towards the tip of your nose.
- *Now you are ready to begin*: Slowly and softly alternate the flapping of your butterfly's wings. Observe your breathing. Bring your

breath down into your abdomen. When you feel comfortable with the rhythm of the fluttering, notice any feelings that arise (pleasure, pain, other physical sensations) and what comes up in your mind (thoughts, images, sounds, odours). Observe, but do not judge the feelings or thoughts. Imagine them as fluffy or dark clouds floating high above you. Let a light breeze push them across the sky, beyond your horizon.

- *For clinicians*: The 'butterfly hug' is a self-administered bilateral stimulation (BLS) method (like the eye movement or tapping) to process traumatic material for an individual or for group work. Desensitization (self-soothing) is a reprocessing by-product using the butterfly hug as BLS (Artigas and Jarero 1998).

 Near and far (Eyes)

This deceptively simple exercise using the eyes can relieve anxiety and introduce a sense of calm.

- *Positioning*: Place a pencil, a pointer (or use your finger) at arm's length and then draw it towards you until your arm is crooked. Draw your attention and your eyes to the tip of the object or your finger. Now look beyond the tip, along an imaginary line, to the furthest point you can find in the room. Move your eyes back and forth between the points (1–3 minutes). Pause, and then repeat the exercise three times.
- *For clinicians*: This is an exercise I learned from my son. According to David Grand, who calls the exercise 'visual convergence', it activates the oculo-cardiac reflex (OCR), functioning as a primitive, powerful and immediate parasympathetic reflex (vagal manoeuvre), rapidly slowing the heart and calming the body[5] (Grand 2013, p.83).

---

5   David Grand hypothesizes that people with repeated losses or instability at an early age in their relationship with their primary caretakers (attachment issues) feel calmer when looking close (when the pointer, or pen or finger, is nearby) and more distressed when they are asked to look off into the distance (2013, p.87).

Humming (Voice and breath)

Humming increases energy, stamina and a sense of wellbeing in a surprisingly short time. Even 10 minutes of humming can make you feel regenerated. I learned to bring humming to a new level during Dhrupad (an ancient genre of Indian classical music) workshops with Uma Lacombe (2017). Humming is a marvellous massage of the inner organs!

- *Positioning*: During Uma's workshops we sat in the lotus position, but any upright position is fine, and hummed or sang for 6 to 7 hours a day. The beneficent effect is as much due to the voice's stimulation of the body as to the changes that occur with rhythmic breathing.
- *For clinicians*: High frequency sounds of about 2000 Hz and higher are stimulating for the brain. Children's voices and most women's voices are high frequency. Other examples include squeaks, a shrill whistle, flute and the higher registers on a violin. Low frequency sounds tire us more easily because we have to block them out to hear the human voice. Low sounds occur at about 500 Hz and lower; some examples of low sounds include: bass drum, tuba, thunder, deep male voice, machines and traffic noise. Humming and singing activate the vagal nerve and correct respiratory, and thus also cardiac and visceral, rhythms (Tomatis 1988, p.63). Singing and playing a wind or brass instrument can produce a similar effect. Short inhalations followed by longer exhalations 'gates the influence of the myelinated vagus on the heart' (Porges 2011, p.254).

Heavenly drum (Ears)

Have you ever been so tired that you cannot fall asleep? An evening in a noisy environment can produce the same sensation. Taoists teach an exercise that simultaneously rests and stimulates the inner ear; they call it 'beating the heavenly drum' (Chang 1986, pp.128–9).

- *Positioning*: Place the index fingers of each hand on the earflaps that allow you to block out sound. Push lightly on the tips of your index fingers until you cut off outside sounds. With the tip of your second finger, tap gently on the finger nails of your index finger. You should hear a metallic sound, similar to the beating of a drum. Tap a slow and regular but steady rhythm (12–36 times). Do three sets of drumming, pausing briefly between each set.

- *For clinicians*: This exercise stimulates and gives rest to the inner ear. On the one hand, the ear needs a rest from hearing sounds that never cease, even when we are asleep. On the other hand, if the inner ear – what Tomatis calls the brain's dynamo (1988) – is too tired, we often have trouble getting to sleep. In 1954, he introduced the concept of a random sonic event or 'electronic gating system' that 'surprises' the muscles of the inner ear; this revitalizes and allows for a restful state (Tomatis 1988, p.127).

 Finger labyrinth (Touch)

A labyrinth is a winding unicursal path leading to a centre. Unlike a maze, the labyrinth does not have traps or blind alleys. Labyrinths are very old. Some date back 4000 years or more. They have long been used symbolically in walking meditation, choreographed dance or as places of ritual and ceremony. The labyrinth evokes metaphor, geometry, pilgrimage. It appears in spiritual practice, environmental art and arenas of social commitment.

Walking through a labyrinth with one's feet, or moving through it with a finger, implies right brain activity. Whenever you feel the need for a break, or the desire to build up your energy or creativity, trace your finger along the white path of this labyrinth to the centre of the circle, pause, then return until you reach the starting point.

Figure 4.1. Labyrinth

Now that you have seen how it works, try alternating your fingers or hands. Synchronizing your breath with the movement of your finger as it moves through the labyrinth can also feel beneficial.

- *For clinicians*: Walking is another example of a self-administered BLS method, which, like eye movement or tapping exercises, is useful for helping process traumatic experiences. During periods of high grief the mourner may feel the need to walk alone but should alternate with accompanied excursions in nature.

CRAFTING THE CEREMONY

Ritualmaking represents a powerful craft that can shape how the bereaved see their loved ones and transform the relationship they shared. Part III looks at the basics of ritual craft: planning, creating and realizing. Like all crafts, ritualmaking requires discipline, creativity, a few guidelines, appropriate tools and a good checklist. Crafting meaningful funeral rituals is a profoundly human activity that involves the mind, the body and even the viscera, a process that takes us to the heart of reality.

5

PLANNING THE CEREMONY

Aaron and his twin sister Audrey were born in the spring, three weeks before term. The doctor congratulated Viviane and Gerry: 'You are the parents of a healthy boy and girl! You'll be home in no time.' Gerry later told Viviane that he'd heard the midwife whisper: 'The girl looks like a Turner baby...' and the doctor retort: 'Nonsense!'

The twins' big sister Gabriela, age five, is overjoyed to have two new poppets to play with. A week after the babies came home, just as they all were settling in to life as a family of five, Audrey turned blue and was rushed to hospital. The diagnosis was congenital heart condition and kidney malformation related to a random chromosomal disorder known as Turner syndrome (TS).[1] The syndrome is a congenital condition that affects only girls; it is not hereditary. Infant mortality for TS is high.[2]

At three weeks of age, Audrey has her first heart operation at a specialized medical centre that is, fortunately, only an hour from their home. The medical staff assures the family that Audrey will be able to live a full life.

Audrey returns to hospital for a week-long routine check-up when she is two and a half years old. Early on a sunny autumn day, Viviane receives a call from Dr Carole, the child's specialist, asking to see both parents as soon as possible. Later that morning, Gerry and Viviane learn that Audrey passed away during the night – and that her death is probably due to a medical error. After apologizing, Dr Carole tells Viviane and Gerry that she believes in open and

---

1   The Turner Syndrome Society (2018) is a reliable source for information about the condition.
2   TS girls who survive are of normal intelligence, but have a variable set of physical challenges that include risk of heart defects, hearing problems, kidney abnormalities, short stature, type 2 diabetes, gluten intolerance, infertility and thyroid disorders. Audrey is missing all of the second chromosome (called full XO Turner syndrome).

honest communication. She encourages them to take their time and to spend as long as they want in the room with their daughter. She says she will accompany them as best she can and kindly gives them her home phone number.

'At the time', Gerry says, 'I couldn't absorb the situation. Then, I angrily imagine that Dr Carole is just doing damage control.' The error is confirmed the next day: Audrey was given at least twice the amount of one of the medications she was intended to have. The attending doctor who wrote up the cardiologist's prescription, without adapting it to her weight, stops by to apologize saying that he hopes that, one day, the family will be able to forgive him. 'The rest of that day and the next,' Gerry adds, 'nurses and doctors mingled respectfully with our friends and family. Even the cleaners stopped to look in on Audrey and ask if we would like the floor swept, water for the flowers, cushions, blankets, coffee or food.'

'It soon became clear to us that Audrey's death didn't just affect our family,' recounts Viviane, 'but her care team as well. Some of them we knew, some we didn't remember. Most of them discreetly touched Audrey's hand or adjusted her sheet before leaving the room. Many of them cried with us. That's when we put aside any thoughts we'd had of litigation and decided to ask the care team help us with Audrey's funeral.'

WHAT KIND OF FUNERAL?

In the first days after a death, people nearly always feel disoriented, particularly when it comes to arranging the funeral.[3] Feelings of grief, sorrow, sadness and dispossession are normal, intrinsic even, to bereavement.

The hospital staff understood this and did not push Audrey's parents into making premature decisions. Medical personnel are well placed to understand the hard reality of death, and to know that, once a person

---

3   Nearly every cultural tradition gives mourners time off from ordinary responsibilities
     to deal with their obligations to the dead and to sort through their emotions. This
     period may be measured in days, weeks, months and even years. In a culture where
     time is money – and money is valued over the quality of human life – having the time
     to deal serenely with the aftermath of death seems like a luxury.

has died, time is no longer of the essence. Sirens, urgent care and rushing about are of little consequence. Audrey's doctor did not let purely administrative issues affect the family. Mourners need to stop, take a deep breath, cry, try to eat, let themselves fall into exhausted sleep or rail against the loss. They need a time-out-of-time to imagine life without their loved one.

Even when a death is foreseeable, even where there is a coronach will, family and friends may still need a week or even months to work together on the funeral. Some situations, as when a person has gone missing or the body must be repatriated, may require even more time.

RITUALS THAT MAKE SENSE

Why is it so tempting to let the funeral director or a religious leader work out the funeral ceremony, rather than create rituals that make sense to us? All funerals are composed of a planning and a realizing phase. In the case of a conventional funeral, involvement of mourners is minimal; the work of interpreting the meaning of the occasion has been done for them, usually by an institution that proposes ready-made ceremonies.

When personalization is called for, the bereaved must embark on the time-consuming but rewarding task of making a custom ceremony. Ritualmaking is a three-phase process that reintroduces the creative phase used intuitively by our ancestors to explore the meaning of this transition in their relationship with the deceased.

RITUAL PROFILE AFFECTS RITUAL STRATEGY

Ritual strategy, that is, the decision about which kind of ceremony is most appropriate, is determined by the deceased's ritual profile and practice (see tools in Chapter 4 and Figure 5.1).[4] Whereas a ready-made liturgical funeral will nearly always be a good fit for a person who was a practising

---

4   The ritual strategy for the funeral of a baby or a young child is determined by the shared ritual profile of the bereaved parents (see *Questionnaire on my ritual profile*, Chapter 4). In the case of a teenager or young adult, the parents should consult with their son/daughter's closest friends (see *Inventory on ritual profile for funerals*). Regrettably, these tools cannot sort out ritual strategy in all cases. See also *Notes on funerals for sensitive situations* (Chapter 7).

member of an institution, it may, or may not, be right for people who felt distanced from their religion or culture of origin. A custom-made or humanist ceremony will usually be suitable for a person with *secular* or *alternative* ritual profile.

Viviane and Gerry's ritual strategy is based on their shared *secular* profile. It feels right to them to include the care team in planning the funeral for Audrey. When the bereaved give themselves the time they need, they usually find the process of creating appropriate ritual remarkably healing.

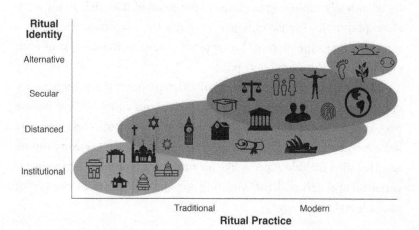

Figure 5.1. Ritual profile

The ritual profiles shown in this graphic take in to account not just people's beliefs and religious affiliation but also their ritual identity and practice. Clarity about one's ritual profile facilitates drawing up a coronach will and determining appropriate ritual strategy for a funeral. The first tool, *Questionnaire on my ritual profile*, helps you understand your own ritual identity and practice. The second tool, *Inventory on ritual profile for funerals*, is designed for determining the best strategy for arranging the funeral of a loved one (see Chapter 4 for both tools).

RITUAL MATERIALS

Contemporary secular ritual is designed around three primal ritual materials: people, participation and place (see centre of Figure 6.1 in

Chapter 6). Everything depends on how a material is used, not on the material itself. Bauhaus architect Ludovic Mies van der Rohe said:

> Each material is only what we make of it. And, just as we acquaint ourselves with materials, just as we must understand functions,[5] so we must become familiar with the psychological and spiritual factors of our day. No cultural activity is possible otherwise; for we are dependent on the spirit of our time.[6] (Mies van der Rohe 1938)

Swiss architect Peter Zumthor[7] builds on the work of Mies van der Rohe by relentlessly exploiting the sensory potential of materials in his work. He explains that 'sense emerges' through the materials. Meaning is not intrinsic to the material but appears unique in the context of each construction (Zumthor 2006, p.10).

In the same way, the crafting of efficient funeral rituals is also a cultural activity that depends on the spirit of our time and how we use people, participation and place. Meaning is not intrinsic to these elements but emerges through the materials. As in architecture, sensory inputs in ritual also include aspects like air movement, odours, temperature variation and natural light. Meaning appears unique in the context of each funeral ceremony.

People

People represent the source of the words, gestures and objects that

---

5   The ideas Ludovic Mies van der Rohe (1886–1969) promoted were not new. Carlo Lodoli (1690–1761), an Italian architectural theorist and mathematician, anticipated modernist notions of functionalism and truth to materials. Mies's genius came from his ability to adapt these notions to the spirit of his time. His architectural forms and proportions were in harmony with the abilities of the materials he used.

6   We are reminded again of cultural psychologist Batja Mesquita's concept of *emotion acculturation*, which contributes to understanding how one set of thoughts and emotions can be replaced by another set, thus keeping us in the spirit of our time (Mesquita *et al.* 2016).

7   Zumthor sees architecture as a form of resistance in a society that celebrates the inessential.

make the funeral meaningful. Each speaker adds to our sense of who the deceased was and what she or he valued. Just because a person has an important role in your father's company does not mean that he is the right person to speak at the funeral. Rituals may be carried out by one person or hundreds of people; it is essential that their words and acts contribute to the sense of the ceremony.

Participation

Participation may be active or passive. People participate in a funeral ceremony through their presence and their through shared experience. Objects that represent or are associated with the deceased also participate in the emergence of meaning. Our sense of this meaning is interpreted through bodily perception (sight, sound, smell, touch and even taste).

Place

The suitability of a place depends on ritual strategy. The physical setting of the ceremony is more than just a space. It serves as a framework for the ceremony and holds the assembly. When choosing a place, consider time and timing as well as availability, the arrangement of the seating and even how the place smells. Find an alternative if the venue does not allow enough time for the ceremony or feel right. The place should contribute to feeling safe because this in turn influences participation and meaning.

The tools proposed in the three chapters on how to craft ritual are organized in toolboxes that correspond to each one of the three phases of ritualmaking: planning, creating and realizing. They are designed to help relatives and friends to become more intuitive and confident in their decision-making about the funeral.

After Viviane and Gerry determine their ritual profile and strategy, they can move into the planning phase. The checklist in this chapter guides them as they craft the ceremony. Other tools help them choose a celebrant and prioritize. They also need to inform others of the news (see the tool *Announcing a death* and Figure 5.2).

Figure 5.2. Public death announcements
Throughout the world, deaths are announced publicly. The first death notices were
carried by messengers who travelled on foot. In ancient Rome, the Acta Diurna
(Daily Newspaper) included a list of people who had died recently. A woman carrying
an ice cream cornet in Chiavenna, Lombardy, Italy checks for recent deaths on the wall
reserved for obits. Most obituaries now also appear in digital format.

© *Daniel Wütschert, CC BY-SA*

Behind the scenes...

An accident often elicits a deep sense of injustice that exacerbates the
pain of loss and hampers grief. Even successful litigation never rights
a wrong. No court can bring Audrey back. When the justice system
does not fail victims outright, the years of waiting for a judgement
may ruin them, destroy their health and make them feel excluded
from society.

Audrey's medical team show integrity and courage by assuming
their responsibility for the accident that cost her life. By sharing
the family's burden, the team confront their feelings of guilt – and
assuage Audrey's family's grief more effectively than any legal
decision.

PLANNING PHASE

> Quis, quid, quando, ubi, cur, quem ad modum, quibus adminiculis.[8]
> (Hermagoras of Temnos, ca. 100 BCE)

The planning phase involves four of Hermagoras's seven questions: who, what, where and when? This is the time for brainstorming. The decisions made during the planning phase are tested for consistency and confirmed during the creating phase. Even if Gerry and Viviane are sure that they want Audrey's doctor to speak at her funeral, they should note down a few other names. What the doctor intends to say must reflect what they need to hear in that context. They need to hear healing words, not a speech that justifies or minimizes her team's error. The parents should feel free to change their minds and ask someone else to speak. An extra step that confirms these decisions appears in the creating phase. It represents a safeguard to ensure that the choices correspond to the needs of the family and all present.

RISK FACTORS FOR THE PLANNING PHASE

The greatest risk in this first phase lies in unexpressed, and thus unmet, expectations. Misunderstandings are often due to lack of communication or to giving people unsuitable roles. Leave time for the unexpected. Make contingency plans for inclement weather.

---

8   Hermagoras of Temnos, a first-century Greek rhetorician, is said to have used the method of dividing a topic into its 'seven circumstances' (who, what, when, where, why, in what way, by what means). His approach inspired the '5 Ws' used widely in journalism, education and police investigation.

TOOLBOX

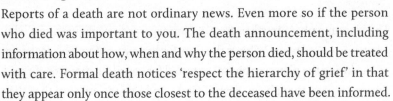

TOOLS FOR THE PLANNING PHASE

Announcing a death

Reports of a death are not ordinary news. Even more so if the person who died was important to you. The death announcement, including information about how, when and why the person died, should be treated with care. Formal death notices 'respect the hierarchy of grief' in that they appear only once those closest to the deceased have been informed.

Informal announcements

If you are responsible for announcing a death, inform the closest friends and relatives as soon as possible so that they do not hear the news from outside sources. Avoid doing it in an impersonal manner. One never knows what such intimate news might mean to another person. A young woman flipped out when she learned of her grandmother's death in a text message, which she read as she was walking down the street. Whenever possible, deliver the news face to face or in a telephone conversation. Hearing the warmth and emotion of a human voice anchors shared sorrow in reality. Here are a few pointers:

- Follow the lead of the closest relatives.
- Support chief mourners. Do inform people around you who may not have access to the official news so that they can participate in the funeral.
- Use common courtesy in social media and messages. If someone passed the news of a death to you in a private note, a telephone message or even a text, respond likewise in a private manner. Do not post it on anyone's public Facebook timeline.

Formal announcements

An obituary, obit or death notice is a public announcement of a death that is typically published in a newspaper and/or on related funeral websites;

it remains the official source of information about the death and the funeral. Usually the obit is brief and paid for by the family.

The formal death notice may follow a format established by the newspaper or website or be written up by family or friends. In the case of a public figure, an obituary notice may appear as a full-length article that details the person's life and accomplishments.

In recent years, obituary style has taken a new turn. While most obits remain sober, some are laced with humour, satire, sarcasm or even vengeance. The text may be composed by a sharp-witted journalist, a survivor seeking revenge or even self-written – often as an attempt to have the last word, or laugh.

Basic information for a death notice:

- full name of the deceased (can include maiden name, former married names or nicknames)
- age at time of death (optional)
- date and location of death
- cause of death (optional)
- names of surviving family members and friends (optional)
- details of the funeral/memorial service (public or private); if public, provide date, time and location
- state whether flowers or donations are appropriate; name of organization/charity for donations.

Longer death announcements may include some biographical information (see *Coronach will* in Chapter 4 and *Writing a meaningful text* in Chapter 6).

CHECKLIST FOR A FUNERAL CEREMONY

PLANNING
First things first

☐ We are clear about our objectives for this ceremony

We have identified:

☐ **About whom?** The **deceased**, her/his life and relationships

☐ **By whom?** **Close family and friends** are responsible for **crafting/presiding/organizing**

☐ **With whom?** Who **participates/is invited**

☐ **What?** Funeral

☐ **When?** Determine date/time/duration

☐ **Where?** A suitable place/setting/venue

COMMUNICATION AND CONTINGENCY

☐ We have contacted or invited all ("With whom?") noted above

☐ Participants have approved their roles

☐ If there is **disagreement** about how to proceed we know who makes the final decision

☐ We have contingency plans for When, Where, What

❚❚ PAUSE

CREATING
Making sense (craftspeople)

We, the craftspeople, are agreed on:

☐ **Why and how** we ritualize our loved one's passing

☐ Deceased is at the **HEART ♥** of this ceremony

☐ The deceased's **key values, ideals or philosophy of life** (in the case of a baby, the parents' values)

☐ **Decisions confirmed** (Who, What, When, Where)

☐ If there is disagreement, we have discussed the issues

CONTENT

☐ **Words ♥ Homage + tributes**

☐ **Music**

☐ **Symbols/objects**

☐ **Gesture of separation**

FORMAT

☐ **Entry** into ceremonial space

☐ **Welcome**

☐ **Heart ♥ Homage + tributes**

☐ **Closing/exit** ceremonial space > transition

☐ **Social gathering**

☐ **Choreography/scenography**

☐ **Reminder list**

☐ **We have checked for flow and choreography**

❚❚ PAUSE

REALIZING
Expressing meaning

☐ **Prepare setting** (presider/participants)

☐ **Open ceremony** (presider)

☐ **Ritualizing** (Content + Format)
 ♦ Conduct (presider) ♦ Participate (all)

☐ **Close ceremony** (presider)

☐ **Open social part of event** (presider)

☐ **Social gathering** (all)

☐ **Close event and clean up** (organizer)

DURATION OF EVENT (suggested)

Ceremony (20–50 minutes)

Social gathering (1–3 hours)

This checklist is not intended to be comprehensive. Modifications to fit specific situations are encouraged.

Copyright © Jeltje Gordon-Lennox 2020

There is something remarkably reassuring about lists. Lists appear simple, often deceptively so. A child can use a list to pick up things for his parents from the corner store. Students, business people, factories and bus companies use agendas, schedules or some form of a timetable to keep track of commitments and deadlines. A person with a failing memory can follow a list to remind herself of her daily routine.

Checklists are required for success, affirms surgeon Atul Gawande (2011, p.79). He distinguishes between three kinds of problems: the simple, the complicated and the complex.

Whether one is building a basic bookcase, a complicated rocket to go to the moon or a complex skyscraper, Gawande insists that the really important things in life should not be left to memory, or to chance.

Under conditions of complexity such as landing an aircraft, operating on a heart or ritualizing a life event, checklists are not optional for success. The *Checklist for a funeral ceremony* undergirds the three-phase creative process of ritualmaking proposed in this book. It helps keep mourners on track. This checklist got one family to fix their attention on writing the homage and put aside – at least until after the funeral – the hurt caused by their father's favouritism.

While a checklist is no substitute for common sense and skill, and it does not list everything one should do, it does guide the designated craftspeople as they identify what is at the heart of the funeral ceremony. It obliges everyone to pause and reflect. The true beauty of the checklist lies in how it makes it possible for people to communicate and assume responsibility – and credit – for the end results.

READ–DO checklists

The list used in this practical guide is referred to as a READ–DO checklist. Each of the three columns in the checklist evokes an action in the crafting process: plan, create (see Chapter 6) and realize (see Chapter 7).

The essential elements are identified, listed and then put together in a certain order.

Function of funeral ceremony checklist

1. *Identify the essential elements* and accomplish the main steps needed to plan, create and realize the ceremony.
2. *Enforce pauses* during which the craftspeople talk to each other about what is at the heart of the occasion *for them*.
3. *Help* those working on the ceremony to (a) *feel like a team* in the creative process, (b) *decide together in advance* what to do and (c) *determine* together *who takes control if things do not go as planned*.
4. Ensure that other *lists are made and used* (e.g. list of items to prepare for the ceremony: objects used, programme, flowers).

Risk factors in using a checklist

While the efficacy of the checklist has been proved time and again, using checklists seems to go against a myth about how successful people function: the truly great are daring; they improvise, they do not need protocols and checklists. 'Maybe our idea of heroism needs updating,' concedes Gawande (2011, p.173). Checklists do impose restrictions: they require personal initiative, discipline and humility. On the upside, lists allow for autonomy and a sense of security in complex situations. In the case of a funeral, the security of a checklist helps craftspeople relax and experience the healing effects of the funeral rituals. Use the checklist. A checklist only works if it is used.

 Who presides?

Hiring a professional is recommended for funerals. As a rule of thumb, do not preside the funeral of someone really close to you. Presiding a ceremony involves signifiant emotional strain, even for professionals. Having someone you trust hold the framework of the ceremony leaves you free to fully mourn your loss. Whether the person who presides at the ceremony is a professional or an amateur, the goal is to ensure that the deceased remains at the centre of the funeral and that the ceremony proceeds as planned (see Figure 5.2 and Table 5.1).

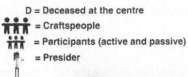

D = Deceased at the centre
= Craftspeople
= Participants (active and passive)
= Presider

Figure 5.2. Roles at a funeral
The deceased is at the centre of the funeral. Craftspeople have a major role in the planning and creation of the ceremony. Participants are witness to the person's transition to a new state. The presider has two main roles: provide a safe context for the expression of strong emotion, and facilitate the physical separation of the participants and the deceased.

The professional's role

The accompaniment of a professional celebrant is particularly constructive in the planning and creating phases. An experienced celebrant will ensure that the script for the ceremony is complete, the format is clear and the scenography is worked out in detail. If there is no professional available for these first two phases the craftspeople must work together, using the tools in this guide. Aim for a sense of your collective relationship with the deceased. If you do not have access to a professional, ask a friend or an acquaintance who is more distantly affected by the death to preside at the ceremony.

Professional support is recommended for all three phases in the following cases:

- there is open or smouldering conflict among the chief mourners
- the chief mourners' experience of the deceased is radically different from her or his public image
- the deceased's ritual profile is *institutional* and *traditional* (call on a religious leader)
- the deceased was *distanced* from religious institutions (determine whether to call on a religious leader or a celebrant).

Basic tips for choosing a presider

- *Do your homework.* Decide exactly what you need and what you want the person you are considering to do: accompany you in the planning and creating phases? Conduct the ceremony? All three? (see Table 5.1).
- *Be wary of giving this responsibility to anyone who might steal the show* (professional or nonprofessional).
- *Before hiring a professional*: (1) Check their professional training, accreditation and celebrant network. (2) Clear up as many questions as possible by telephone or email (availability, services offered, extra fee for distance if travel is required).
- *During the interview*: (1) Ask the celebrant to run through the process of crafting a ceremony. (2) How is the content of the ceremony determined? (If the professional supplies a set script, you will work less but *you will not* get a custom ceremony.) (3) Ask for details about what the rate covers (limit on number of meetings, telephone or email exchanges? On-site rehearsal?).
- *Hire only a celebrant who fits your basic criteria* (good first impression, professionalism, availability). Fees vary greatly from region to region. As with most services, the least expensive is not always the best choice. Experienced professionals who help their clients craft bespoke ceremonies must charge higher rates; typically they invest 20–40 hours in accompaniment and presiding a funeral ceremony.

Most offer a follow-up session within a year of the ceremony at no extra charge.

- *Trust your instincts!*

The person you choose to preside the funeral must be able to put the focus on you and your objectives for the ceremony, provide timely advice and support you unconditionally on this special occasion.

The columns in Table 5.1 present two roles along with the goals and requirements one might expect from the person presiding a funeral ceremony.

TABLE 5.1. WHAT DOES PRESIDING INVOLVE?

	Professional celebrant	Amateur artisan
GOAL	Professional accompaniment in the creation and performance of meaningful funeral rituals	Amateur accompaniment of friends/family as they create and perform meaningful funeral rituals
REQUIREMENTS		
Professional training	Hands-on celebrant training and experience required	Experience is an advantage
Public speaking	Experience required; ability to hold and make an audience feel safe	Experience is an advantage
Role	Supportive leadership and accompaniment. Preside funeral	Accompaniment. Preside funeral
Approach	Professional client-centred service (*priority: clients' needs and goals*)	Disciplined accompaniment (*honesty about own limits*)
Values expressed	Respect for the deceased's values	Respect for the deceased's values
Presence	Calm	Reassuring
Reasonable expectations	Conduct ceremony with sensitivity. Deal efficiently with unexpected incidents. Remuneration for service	Conduct the ceremony. Unpaid volunteer service

Prioritizing

This tool helps visualize what is most important to you, whether that be the choice of a venue or a presider. You can use it alone or with the team of craftspeople. Prioritizing helps you make decisions about who to invite, where to hold the ceremony and who participates. It takes about 20 minutes.

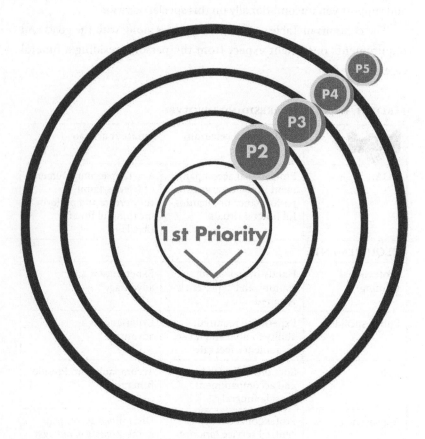

Figure 5.3. How to prioritize
This tool is useful for determining your priorities.

Materials needed

Enlargement of Figure 5.3, writing materials and tracing paper.

First round

This round is about *expectations* – yours and others. Place tracing paper on top of Figure 5.3. Place the names of the people you are *expected* to be close to, or options you think you *should* choose in P1 – this represents your inner circle or top choices and priorities. P2 is your second circle. Place less important people and options in sections P3, P4 and P5. Take a picture of the diagram and label it 'Version A'.

Second round

This round is about *feelings*. Identify the people or options you *feel* good about. Take a picture and label it 'Version B'. If this version resembles Version A, you know that you are on the right track. Skip the third round. You are ready to make your choices. If your versions are quite different, take it to another round.

Third round

This round is about *compromise*. Obligations, budget, what we want and what we need do not always match up. Compare versions A and B. What is it about this person or that choice that makes it difficult for you decide? What creative solutions are there for your situation?

Example 1: Roles at the funeral

It falls to you to organize your gay uncle's funeral. Your mother and aunt want to help but are making your job difficult. Where do these people figure in the organization of the funeral? The distribution of roles becomes clearer when you see where you have placed each protagonist. Your uncle's partner is with you in P1. Your mother is in P2. Your homophobic aunt, who never accepted her brother's choices, is in P3. You and your uncle's partner compose the team of craftspeople. You ask your mother to speak about her relationship with her brother during the ceremony. The aunt, a graphic artist, happily makes the programme.

Example 2: Funeral venue

The team of craftspeople for your mother's funeral is composed of five people: your father, your brother, your niece, the celebrant and you. You agree that your mother's ritual profile is *secular* and *modern*. Your father says he is too upset to participate actively but wants veto power. The celebrant is there to keep things on track. It's up to your brother, your niece and you to decide about the venue. Collectively, you agree it is important to control costs, have a good sound system, reduce travel distance for participants and introduce a connection to nature. Your mother was an avid gardener who enjoyed being in the open air. Three of the five options put forward in the first round were knocked out in the second round because there was not a consensus about what felt right. In the third round, it came down to a choice between a room at the funeral home where the sound system is excellent or a secular chapel at the green cemetery (with no sound system) where your father also wants to be buried. When you realize that you can hire a sound system and, weather permitting, even have an outdoor ceremony there, the choice is validated by all five members of your team.

 NOTES ON THE PILLARS
OF RITUAL DESIGN

'No design is possible until the materials with which you design are completely understood' (Mies van der Rohe, cited in Borden 2010, p.7). The materials used in ritual design are buttressed by six pillars: a ceremony must meet an identified need, take place in a specific context, with people who assume special roles, the content of the ceremony must make sense and be consistent with the ritual profile and values of the deceased (see Figure 6.1 in Chapter 6).

NEED

The raison d'être of ritualizing is our profound human need.

Most of the time this need is self-evident. Nonetheless, it helps to clarify it early on in the creative process.

CONTEXT

Adequate understanding of context is crucial. Effective ritual is influenced by the impedance of place and time. When these aspects feel right during a ceremony, there is a felt sense that emotions are being contained or held by the context and a felt shift is effected. This is what makes it possible for important concerns or uncertainty to be dealt with by the group. For more on context see *Notes on rules for ritual design* (Chapter 6).

ROLES

Attributing the right roles to the right people requires an accurate grasp of the context. In the case of a funeral ceremony, the life and values of the deceased are at the centre of the rituals crafted by friends and family. Others may participate actively and/or as witnesses to the funeral. The presider's role is to hold the frame so that emotion can be expressed safely (see Figure 5.2).

CONTENT

Elements such as meaningful words, gestures, music and objects constitute the content of a ceremony. This content unpacks and conveys to those present who and what is at the heart of the ritual. All artistic elements should contribute to these aims of the funeral.

SENSEMAKING

Ritualizing death and loss meets our fundamental human need to make sense of what is happening to and around us. Making ritual that feels right involves *seeking, creating* and *taking* meaning (Holloway 2015). Mourners *seek* meaning through their choices about the different aspects of the funeral ceremony, such as venue and content, including music, readings, dress, object, symbols, who participates and who is invited. These elements *express* meaning which those present *take* from the ceremony as they mark the transition and anchor it in their daily lives.

COHERENCE

Coherence is the glue that holds the elements of the ritual together. There is consistency when (1) need and expectations are clear, (2) the roles are played by the right people, (3) in the right context, (4) expressed with suitable content and (5) that conveys meaning (see *Coherence test* in Chapter 6).

Key to the questionnaire on my ritual profile

What is your ritual profile? Being clear about your ritual profile helps you determine your ritual strategy. A coherent strategy is essential for designing, creating and implementing appropriate rituals that celebrate your life events.

These symbols ★ ● ■ ◆ are indicators of your ritual profile.

★   (5)* **Institutional**. If this symbol ★ represents the majority of your answers, your religious practice is regular and satisfying. A religious ceremony would be important for you and consistent with your values and view of life. You probably also ticked this symbol ✣.

●   (5) **Distanced**. A majority of this symbol ● indicates occasional religious practice; your ties with a religious institution maybe stretched. A ceremony held with a religious leader in a traditional setting may or may not satisfy your need to mark a life event. You may also have ticked the symbol ★. A clear majority of this symbol ✣ indicates a personalized religious ceremony would be appropriate; a majority of this symbols ▲ points to a personalized ceremony outside a religious context.

■   (6) **Secular or Humanist**. A majority of this symbol ■ indicates that you identify yourself as a 'none' (e.g. atheist, agnostic). You may be indifferent or even against religion. You may be a member of a humanist or secular group. Tailor-made or humanist ceremonies would best serve your need to mark a life event. You may have a majority of either of these symbols ▲ ✣.

◆   (5) **Alternative**. If you ticked this symbol ◆ at least three times it means you find yourself most comfortable with a holistic approach to life and may be a member of an esoteric group. A bespoke ceremony would suit you well. If you ticked a majority of this symbol ▲ consider an alternative to a ceremony presided by a traditional authority figure.

These two symbols ▲ ❖ about practice help you fine-tune your ritual profile.

❖   (4) **Traditional**. Cultural and social activities linked to one or more traditions are important to your sense of identity. Yet, feeling strong ties with a tradition neither precludes nor indicates a desire for custom ritual or ceremony. However, when a ritualizing an occasion, you may need to hear some traditional phrases or to perform certain traditional gestures. It is likely that you ticked a number of these symbols ★ ● ■, but improbable that you have a majority of this symbol ◆.

▲   (5) **Modern**. You feel comfortable with people who respect your personal journey and who encourage you in the development of your own values. You may belong to groups with little official status and avoid institutional settings. It is important that you feel free to craft the kind of rituals that are right for you. While you may have ticked a number of these symbols ● ■ ◆, it is unlikely that you have a majority of this symbol ★.

Indicates the maximum number of times this symbol appears in the questionnaire.

Key to the inventory on ritual profile for funerals

These symbols ★ ● ■ ◆ are indicators of *how you perceive* your family member or friend's ritual profile.

★   (5)* **Institutional**. If this symbol ★ represents the majority of your answers, you see your family member or friend as having had a religious practice that was regular and probably satisfying. A religious funeral with a religious leader in a traditional setting would be coherent with his/her values and view of life. You probably also ticked this symbol ❖ a few times.

●   (5) **Distanced**. A majority of this symbol ● indicates that you perceive your family member or friend's religious practice as occasional. Her/his ties with a religious institution may have been stretched. A funeral held in a religious setting may or may not be the best way to honour her/his life. A personalized religious ceremony is indicated if you also ticked the symbol ★ and see a clear majority of this symbol ❖. A majority of this symbol ▲ points to the need for a personalized non-religious funeral.

■   (6) **Secular or Humanist.** A majority of this symbol ■ indicates that you identify your family member or friend as a 'none' (e.g. atheist, agnostic). S/he may have been indifferent or even against religion. Perhaps s/he was a member of a humanist or secular group. A custom or humanist funeral ceremony would most likely best honour her/his life. You may have ticked a majority of either of these symbols ▲ ✣.

◆   (5) **Alternative.** If this symbol ◆ was ticked at least three times it means you see your family member or friend as having been most comfortable with a holistic approach to life. S/he may have been a member of an esoteric group. A bespoke funeral ceremony would best honour her/his life. If you ticked a majority of this symbol ▲ consider an alternative to a funeral presided by a traditional authority figure.

These two symbols ▲ ✣ help you fine-tune how you see your family member or friend's ritual practice.

✣   (4) **Traditional.** You see cultural and social activities linked to one or more traditions as having been important to your family member or friend's sense of identity. Strong ties with tradition do not necessarily mean one should organize a religious funeral. However, it does mean that it is important to include some traditional phrases or gestures in the funeral. It is likely that you ticked a number of these symbols ★ ● ■; a majority of this symbol ◆ is improbable.

▲   (5) **Modern.** You perceive the personal journey and values of your family member or friend as being of utmost importance. S/he may have belonged to groups with little official status and avoided institutional settings. A funeral with crafted rituals would probably best reflect her/his life, values and interests. While you may have ticked a number of these symbols ● ■ ◆, it is unlikely you have a majority of this symbol ★.

* Indicates the maximum number of times this symbol appears in the inventory.

How do you *perceive* your family member or friend's ritual profile? Your results represent the jumping-off point for discussion about a ritual strategy for the funeral. Agreement on ritual profile and a joint ritual strategy is essential for designing, creating and implementing appropriate funeral rituals for your loved one.

CREATING THE CEREMONY

On the second day after Audrey's death, Viviane and Gerry speak with Dr Carole about including the staff in Audrey's funeral and having it at the hospital. Surprised and moved, she offers to talk with the board of directors. 'They may well refuse to cooperate,' Dr Carole says. 'If that's the case, enough of the staff is ready to work with you on this in another setting. You have my word and my support.'

That afternoon, Susan, a professional celebrant, joins the family and a few staff members in Audrey's room to begin making plans. Gabriela sets the tone when she exclaims: 'Audrey will never have another birthday party with Aaron. We have to give her one, now!' Since they expect that a number of children will attend, Viviane and Gerry envisage a short ceremony followed by games, party food and Audrey's favourite hospital clowns.

The hospital board's first reaction is to put off making a decision about the ceremony and to sack the doctor responsible for the error that lead to Audrey's death. The family protests the sacking and moves Audrey's body to a funeral parlour. With the support of Dr Carole and Susan, they continue planning for the funeral at the family's home. After the head nurse and the hospital pharmacist join the small group, the organization of the ceremony falls into place rather quickly. The biggest obstacle remains finding the right venue.

On a Wednesday, two weeks after Audrey's death, the family and Dr Carole present the board with their plans for the funeral. The board responds by offering the family the use of the hospital cafeteria and the garden area at the weekend, on the condition that the ceremony and the activities planned for Audrey's funeral are not open to the public. Both the family and the hospital agree not to contact the press. The date and time for the funeral is set for Sunday during hospital visiting hours, from 3 to 5 o'clock in the afternoon.

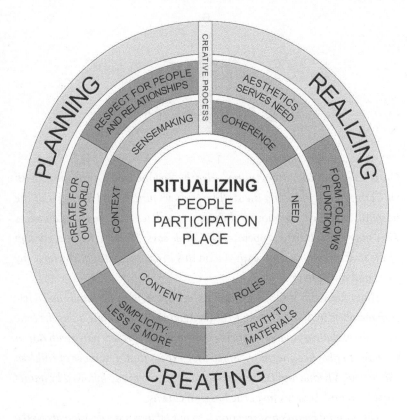

Figure 6.1. Creative process
The three phases of the creative process appear in the outer ring (planning, creating, realizing) and the main materials at the heart of the diagram (people, participation and place). Six words form the pillars of ritual design (see *Notes* in Chapter 5) and six short phrases represent the rules for ritualmaking (see *Notes* in this chapter). This figure is based on an original diagram made by Walter Gropius for the Bauhaus curriculum, which combines theory with practical training and an apprenticeship programme, much like a good celebrant training programme.

A wide variety of rituals are practised around death and fear of loss. A mother knits a symbol of protection into her baby's bonnet and, in the process, takes the edge off her fear of losing the child to an early death. A mourner eases his experience of loss by composing a threnody that honours the memory of his beloved spouse. Victims of negligence initiate a lawsuit to obtain recognition of their suffering, symbolic reparation and social reintegration. Listening to just the right music at a funeral ceremony helps the bereaved mourn the loss of their loved one. These four activities may be referred to as superstition, making art, appealing to the justice system and ceremony. Together they represent a spectrum of ritual activity (see Figure 3.3 in Chapter 3) that involves an incessant shifting back and forth between thoughts or concepts and embodied gestures or objects.

RITUALMAKING: A CREATIVE PROCESS

Although we have little explicit knowledge of how our ancestors invented their rituals, it is clear that then, as now, ritual was constituted of art-filled activity. The amazing capacity of the human imagination to produce and embody abstract signs is crucial to the creative process of ritualmaking. Although imagination is fundamental to human creativity (Tateo 2015), we often think of it as something irrational or unreal: 'He just *imagined* it.'

In fact, imagination is a rather specific form of adaptive behaviour that allows us to project ourselves into the future. This projection may result in our becoming more, or less, fearful. When people sense that their fears are recognized and understood, they may feel safer and shift out of disorganized states. A kind face or gesture can invite a gut feeling of safety – communicated from viscera to brain and mind – and effect a radical shift in behaviour in the face of uncertainty (Porges 2020).

The kind encouragement of Pliny's uncle's friends, along with his ability to imagine safety, pushed him to flee with his mother from the volcanic fallout. Through intentionality, expressivity and creativity Pliny made sense of and managed his feelings of confusion and insecurity. Later, he used these same processes to nourish his spirit with art-filled activities (Chapter 1).

TIE CREPE BOWS ON PUBLIC DOVES[1]

Meaningful rituals rely on intentionality, expressivity and the creative process. Why is it so important to reclaim our creative power? Journalist and author Brenda Ueland answers: 'Because there is nothing that makes people so generous, joyful, lively, bold and compassionate, so indifferent to fighting and the accumulation of objects and money' (2010 [1938], p.155).

Ceremonial ritual, in particular, represents a prime opportunity to develop and display the arts in society. 'In fact', says ethologist Ellen Dissanayake, 'it is hard to imagine what would constitute a ceremony [without art]' (2017, p.155). The creative process of ritualmaking is what sets emerging ritual apart from stock ceremonies.

When the human imagination is solicited in a safe setting, the creative processes of ritualmaking and ritual practice can transform ordinary symbols and objects into something extraordinarily beneficial. We ritualize for many reasons, not the least of which is to feel safe. 'What would it be like if creative people felt safe, or...more people could become creative if they felt safe?' asks neuroscientist Stephen W. Porges (2012).[2]

Even more astonishing is how the interplay between the individual and collective imagination allows human beings to enhance both self- and social regulation (Tateo 2016, p.50).

---

1   The crepe bow refers to a band of black silk or imitation silk, formerly tied around a person's hat or arm as a sign of mourning. This heading alludes to the third line of the second paragraph of W.H. Auden's poem 'Funeral Blues' (1940, p.91).

2   Stephen W. Porges's work helps us understand how dynamic our biological systems are. He explains why a kind face and a soothing tone of voice can dramatically alter the entire organization of the human organism – that is, how being seen and understood can help shift people out of disorganized fearful states. If physiological communication from viscera to brain and mind is the royal road to affect regulation, this invites a radical shift in our approach in the use of ritual for healing trauma and for dealing with grief (Porges 2011, 2020).

Grimes: Ritualizing with our own stuff

Some rituals are not much more than sugary confections, all tantalization and immediate gratification, but ultimately leaving us starved for real meaning. Pilfering other people's rituals can turn into a spiritual imperialism that mirrors Western culture's historic sense of ownership of the world. One of the reasons we might become interested in the rituals of hunter-gatherer societies is because we are moving around a lot, like hunters and gatherers. But our sense of connection with space and our sense of loyalty to a particular place have changed; our ritual sensibility has changed as well.

Like traditional rituals, do-it-yourself (DIY) ritual can result in complicity, empty gestures, people having to do something they resist doing. In either case, deep-seated resentment can lie under the surface of ritual acts. If DIY rituals are really going to meet our needs, they have to be made up out of the familiar, not the exotic: metaphors that make sense to us, language that reflects the way we see the world, and symbols with which we have a history. Start with your own broken teacups, the stuff in your backyard, keepsakes in the backs of drawers. Begin there, not with someone else's rituals. (Ronald Grimes, personal communication 2016)

Behind the scenes...

Viviane and Gerry learn that the hospital administration intend to discipline Dr Carole for insubordination and to dismiss the doctor responsible for the error that took Audrey's life. When they discover that this doctor had been working 36 hours straight – and that his schedule is considered 'normal' at the hospital – they feel compelled to lend their moral weight to the staff's efforts to change the situation. It took threats about involving the media to convince the administration to assume a more humane personnel policy.

CREATING PHASE

The creating phase of ritualmaking addresses Hermagoras's three questions not included in the planning phase: why, how, by what means? Why are you ritualizing this occasion? How do you imagine it? What means will you use? As noted earlier, the creation phase is superfluous to ready-made ceremonies,[3] but essential to handcrafted ritual.

Take your time. You may begin with ideas of what the funeral ceremony should look like. Set them aside and imagine how you would like it to be. Maybe what you create will be totally different from anything you have seen elsewhere, or maybe it will be similar. Creation is not about *giving* the occasion meaning or what it *should* mean; it is about uncovering *what it means to you*. Gloria Steinem tells us to 'create the means that best reflect the ends we want. Try to make each moment authentic, and you'll get to an authentic end' (2012, n.p.). The goal is not originality, or even beauty, but simplicity, truthfulness and authenticity.

RISK FACTORS FOR THE CREATING PHASE

It is tempting to buy a pile of books or spend hours on the internet to see what others wrote or what funeral rituals they used. Trust yourself. Have a look at how others went about it, but only after you have decided what you want to write or do. Most people find their choices confirmed. Avoid introducing surprises at a funeral. Improvised tributes, in particular, often prove confusing, overwhelming or tiresome. They are welcome at an informal reception after the funeral.

---

3   Most religious and civil leaders are ill equipped to deal with requests for personalization. Uninformed attempts to personalize a stock ceremony, often with elements that are cut and pasted from other cultures, have justifiably led to severe criticism of do-it-yourself.

TOOLBOX

TOOLS FOR THE CREATING PHASE

Why and how?

This exercise facilitates brainstorming about why you are ritualizing this occasion and how you imagine the ceremony. Alone you may go faster but as a group you may go farther. This exercise should take no more than 15 minutes.

Materials needed

A sheet of paper and writing tools for each person, plus one extra sheet for the group discussion.

Questions

Craftspeople should first work separately on the questions below. Note down the answers that come readily. Follow your gut feelings.

- *Why* is this occasion important to me? What do I want to convey? (Keep it down to 3–5 words, e.g. my respect for my father.)
- *How* do I envisage the ceremony? What do I NOT want to see, hear or do?

If you are working alone, you may want to check your answers with a good friend, therapist, celebrant or coach before moving on to the next tasks in this phase.

If you are fortunate enough to be working as a team, share your ideas about why and how. Set aside judgement and listen to each person's ideas. Now ask: What do we want to convey as a group through this ceremony? Identify (1) which aspects are clear to all and (2) where negotiation is needed. Have we taken into account group discussions? The needs of different members of the group? Tackle the areas that require negotiation and make a final version. Once you have agreement on what you want to convey, you have finished the exercise and can move on to the next tasks.

Core values

This tool is useful in identifying the deceased's central values as demonstrated in her or his life and relationships (see suggestions for core values in Table 6.1).

Note the words, phrases, objects, memories that come to mind when you think of the deceased. Let's say you chose three words: beauty – generosity – security. While one person may see beauty as an aesthetic sense, another may think only of physical attractiveness. Generosity can bring up a rich feeling of giving or evoke receiving. Security may mean money in the bank or strong locks on windows and doors. The same applies to the meanings you give to three objects that remind you of the deceased: favourite hat – book – food. These elements represent the deceased's core values. The significance of these elements and their relationship to the deceased will undoubtedly differ from one person to the next.

Imagine a circumstance or story that goes along with this word or item. Some things are fine for a public setting; other anecdotes or stories may be more private. You now have what you need to structure a thematic homage as a group or to compose a tribute from your unique vantage point through an anecdote, music, poetic language or expressive movement.

TABLE 6.1. TERMS EXPRESSING CORE VALUES

Accepting	Accommodating	Adventurous
Affectionate	Agreeable	Allegiance
Alluring	Altruistic	Ambitious
Analytical	Appreciative	Articulate
Artistic	Assertive	Attentive
Authentic	Balanced	Beauty
Broad-minded	Calm	Candid
Careful	Cheerful	Clever
Comforting	Commitment	Communicative
Compassionate	Competent	Conscientious
Cooperative	Courageous	Creative
Curiosity	Decisive	Dependable

Devoted	Dignity	Diplomatic
Discreet	Easy-going	Educated
Effective	Efficient	Encouraging
Elegance	Empathy	Entertaining
Enthusiastic	Excellence	Exploration
Fairness	Family	Fidelity
Flexibility	Forgiving	Forthright
Freedom	Friendship	Frugal
Generous	Genuine	Good sport
Good-tempered	Gracious	Grateful
Happiness	Hard-working	Harmony
Helpful	Honest	Honourable
Hopeful	Humane	Humble
Humorous	Imaginative	Industrious
Inquisitive	Insightful	Integrity
Intelligence	Intuitive	Joy
Justice	Kindness	Knowledge
Leadership	Love	Loyalty
Maturity	Mindfulness	Modesty
Motivation	Obedience	Open-mindedness
Openness	Optimism	Order
Originality	Passion	Peace
Perceptive	Perfection	Piety
Pleasure	Pleasant	Polite
Power	Practicalness	Pragmatism
Precision	Professionalism	Purity
Quick-witted	Realism	Relaxation
Reliability	Resourceful	Respectful
Security	Self-control	Self-discipline
Selflessness	Serenity	Service
Sharing	Simplicity	Sincerity

Skilfulness	Sociable	Solidarity
Spirited	Spirituality	Stability
Strength	Support	Sympathy
Tactful	Talented	Teamwork
Thoughtful	Tidy	Tolerant
Truthful	Trust	Understanding
Unity	Valour	Well-mannered
Well-spoken	Wisdom	

 Two inboxes

The inboxes represent an organizational tool that structures the work of the creative phase (see Figure 6.2). It helps craftspeople keep track of the elements that are needed, have been received or are still outstanding so they can order them in a suitable format.

Content

- Homage (text)
- Personal tributes (texts, acts, music, art forms)
- Opening and closing words
- Music (ceremony)
- Gestures and symbols
- Decorations (if applicable)

Format

- Beginning (entry, welcome)
- Middle (homage, tributes, gestures, symbols)
- End (closing, exit)

Figure 6.2. Inboxes for keeping track of content and format

Content

Primal ritual materials for your ceremony include people, participation and place (see centre of Figure 6.1). The content of the ceremony is composed of words, music, objects and gestures. A succinct homage and four to five tributes from people who represent different areas of the deceased's life round out a ceremony nicely. Ensure that these elements are coherent with the life and values of the deceased (see *Coherence test*).

If you intend to distribute a programme, include the names of people who participate in the order of ceremony. In the case of a group presentation, note the name of the group (e.g. handball club, tutoring association, choir); the names of members may be listed elsewhere in the programme.

Format

Once you have most of the content of the ceremony, take stock of the different elements, put them in the most logical order and compose a first draft.

Timing

Build in the concept of time during this phase. Imagine the contributors speaking and performing the envisaged gestures. How will they feel to you and the assembly on the day of the ceremony? How long are the different elements? Keep tributes concise. Does the *tone* of the ceremony feel right to you? Let your ideas settle and come back to this point again later.

A well-structured and presided ceremony will show the deceased to best advantage (20–50 minutes). The length of a ceremony is not an indication of your love and respect for the deceased nor of her or his importance to society (see *Checklist for a funeral ceremony*).

 Writing a meaningful text

The dandelion clock model (see Figure 6.3) represents a simple structure for funeral texts. The model is based on a chronological homage (stem) or eulogy that forms the storyline. From a mere seed the dandelion grows into a mature flower. Its yellow head soon transforms into a white sphere called a clock (or blowball). Dandelion clocks are composed of seeds (achenes). The personal tributes (seeds) – often unconnected stories – illustrate different facets of the deceased's life. The seeds are connected to a tuft of fine hairs designed to separate the seed from the stem and promote new change. The tributes too presage a radical change in the relationship. As the wind tugs on the hairs, it disperses the seeds over long distances and fosters the emergence of new life.

Homage

The homage might also be compared to the storyline of a good television series where each episode, with its ups and downs, builds up to the last one that then closes the season. The series does not necessarily have a happy ending, but it does clarify the deceased's core values and relationships. The homage brings the deceased's life into focus by highlighting significant events, achievements and relationships in a chronological or thematic order. While chronological order works well for honouring the life of an adult, the thematic approach is useful for a child or young person. The homage is written from a neutral standpoint, usually by several family members and close friends. Read early in the ceremony, it gives the assembly an overview of the deceased's life story and introduces significant people and themes.

In the case of a 98-year-old whose cronies had all preceded him in death, the family decided to honour their patriarch with a ceremony composed of his amateur paintings and an homage that served as a lesson in the family's genealogy. His grandchildren and great-grandchildren each received a souvenir copy of the text.

These points may be covered in an homage:

- full name (also name before marriage, if applicable)
- date and place of birth
- childhood: family home, childhood friends and memories
- education/vocational training: schools, internships, graduation, diplomas
- family life: parents, siblings, godmother, godfather, marriage(s), children, grandchildren...

- experience: professional, volunteer, military service
- interests: sports, hobbies, entertainment, reading, travel, art, languages, spirituality, knowledge of specialized fields
- ties: family, close friendships
- memberships in organizations, including religious, civic, cultural, fraternal
- values, human qualities
- date and place of death
- disposal of body (burial, green burial, cremation, other)
- location of 'final resting place'.

The homage should contain a reference to the people doing tributes so that assembly can place them, or the organization they represent, in context.

Figure 6.3. Dandelion clocks and storytelling
The dandelion clock model is based on the anatomy of the flower which structures the classic funeral ceremony with multiple speakers. The homage is the stem; the speakers' tributes and other ritual elements are like the seeds clustered at the top of the stem.

Tributes

Tributes reveal different facets of the deceased's life and relationships. They come after the homage and give depth to the deceased's life and relationships. A tribute may be an act, an original short story or poem, a piece of music or art that shows gratitude, respect or admiration.

The most memorable tributes are anecdotes, short stories, significant objects, sounds or even perfumes or flavours that are created especially for the occasion.

A short personal tribute casts light on the deceased's relationship with one person or with a group of people (friends, members of a club, work or volunteer context). If possible, let your text sit for a time (hours or days). Come back to it now and again to ask: Does this fit? Does it feel right? Authenticity and coherence are of the essence.

The presider should present each person doing a tribute by name, along with their ties to the deceased (e.g. brother, schoolmate, cousin).

Just the right music

Music and the other arts are not just decorative; they represent important elements in a funeral service. The natural sounds of distress emitted by humans, and animals, over the death of a loved one may very well be a model for composing and performing public and private funeral laments like the coronach. It is one more way of doing something to relieve feelings of helplessness, individual isolation, despair and anxiety (Dissanayake 2006, pp.34–5). Live music (vocal, instrumental) can have emotional and transformative power when it is performed as tribute that reveals a facet of the deceased's life.

Music sets the mood and enhances meaning in a ceremony. It may also serve as a 'breather' after an intensely emotional moment. The first music that comes to mind when preparing a funeral may be a piece by the deceased's preferred artist or a song that reminds friends and family of her or him. Choose music that fits your goals, corresponds with the core values of the deceased and enhances the meaning of the occasion. It is not customary to applaud after live music at a funeral. Even a funeral for a musician is not a concert or a theatrical performance.

Playing music as the assembly enters and exits the ceremonial space can feel reassuring. The entrance piece should be meditative (not necessarily sombre) to quiet people's uneasiness. The exit piece can be more lively. Music for entrances and exits must be long enough for people to move from one spot to another. Recorded pieces played during the ceremony should be short. Two to three minutes of music can feel very long to mourners.

Logistics

How much music do you need for this funeral? How long are the pieces? Is the music recorded or will it be played by amateur or professional musicians? Where do they fit in the ceremony? Who is responsible for the music on the day of the ceremony? Who will cue the musicians or put the music on at the right time?

Small gestures, big impact

Every culture uses gestures and symbols to mark funerals. Be curious. You may want to investigate the gestures and symbols of the deceased's cultural tradition or origin. While some gestures like lifting a glass in a toast or sharing food are widely understood, others, such as the act of sprinkling water on a coffin, are too closely tied to religious rites to be used with impunity in secular settings. Be wary, too, of misappropriating rituals from other cultures. Let your imagination inspire you to do something (with gestures, songs, objects) that ties in with the core values you have identified. Particularly if you decide to have everyone perform a certain gesture (during leave-taking at the graveside, for example) determine and let people know in advance what the gesture or symbol is intended to express (gratitude, honour, separation).

An indoor ceremonial space offers certain advantages, such as microphone and sound system for playing recorded music, that are difficult to organize in natural settings and at gravesites or columbariums. At a burial, chief mourners are expected to tell the funeral attendant in advance if they want the casket lowered as soon as everyone is gathered or if they should wait until the mourners leave. Choose someone in advance to lead the way with a gesture of separation if the chief mourners think they might want time alone in the cemetery after the burial.

In the case of the artist grandfather mentioned above, the family asked the assembly to file by the paintings displayed in his honour as they left the room. At the columbarium, after their son's urn was placed in the niche, another family asked mourners to sing one of his favourite songs accompanied by a guitarist (lyrics were handed out). At other funerals, the flowers from the floral arrangements or other biodegradable objects were distributed by funeral attendants who then invited the mourners to file by the open grave and toss their symbol on the casket before leaving the cemetery.

 Coherence test

Use the Coherence grid (Table 6.2) to explore how the core values are expressed concretely in each aspect of the funeral.

Pencil your keywords in the top row and compare them with the different aspects of your preparation for the ceremony. Do the elements express the values of the deceased? Have you covered a number of the different facets of her or his life? Is the content of the ceremony balanced?

TABLE 6.2. COHERENCE GRID

	Deceased's values (keywords across)				
Death announcement					
Date/time of ceremony					
Ceremony/reception venue					
Choice of presider, participants					
Homage*					
Tributes* 1, 2, etc.					
Gestures*					
Music*					

Materials used (*tables, chairs, serving, decorations*)					
Disposal of body					
Final resting place					
Cost					
Other					

* see appropriate tool

Format of the ceremony

All ceremonies have a beginning, a middle and an end. The format or order represents the framework for the content (see *Order of a sample funeral ceremony*). The homage is read early on in the ceremony, followed by the tributes – chief mourners usually intervene first. When all the elements are in, place them in the order that makes the most sense to you.

Prepare a one-page chronological order of the ceremony in bullet form. This order of ceremony should contain the names of all of the people who actively participate in order of appearance. In the event of a group presentation (e.g. choir), note the name of the group. Readers, musicians and funeral personnel should be able to see, at a glance, when they intervene.

Once you have the final version of this one-page outline, copy it on to a new document and label it 'Complete version of the ceremony'. Like a libretto, the complete version of the ceremony should contain all the words spoken (full text of participants), and the stage directions (who does what, when, where and how). Complete the names of the people who actively participate with their tie to the deceased. This new document is for the presider and should be approved by the chief mourners/craftspeople. Is what each speaker intends to say appropriate? Does it fit into that time in the ceremony? Do the elements follow in a harmonious and reassuring manner?

When you are satisfied with the format, test out the scenography, in situ if possible. Does the timing work? Consider how to introduce the transition in to the social gathering.

Finally, make a list of all of the elements or objects needed on the day of the ceremony. For good measure, add a list with the telephone numbers of all those involved; don't forget the musicians and the funeral director, if appropriate.

Sample order of a funeral ceremony

BEGINNING
- **Music** – arrival in ceremonial space
- **Welcome** – presider

MIDDLE
- **Homage** – presider
- **Tribute** – close relative
- **Tribute** – friend
- **Music**
- **Tribute** – friend
- **Tribute** – classmate

END
- **Words of closure** – presider
- **Symbolic gesture** – leave-taking
- **Music** – departure from ceremonial space
- **Informal social gathering**

NOTES ON RULES FOR RITUAL DESIGN

Design rules keep the craftspeople on track during the creative process. Design rules also give a basis for evaluating how well the design works. Steve Jobs is quoted as saying:

> Most people make the mistake of thinking design is what it looks like. People think it's this veneer – that the designers are handed this box and told, 'Make it look good!' That's not what we think design is. It's not just what it looks like and feels like. Design is how it works. (cited in Walker 2003)

The first letter of these basic rules for ritual design form the acronym 'CRAFTS'. The rules help craftspeople design rituals that work.

CREATE FOR OUR WORLD

Time-honoured ritual elements – such as water or salt – do not in and of themselves communicate meaning in funerary rituals. Rituals that we create or adapt to our world and context have the power to honour the past and transform our future relationships. In the case described below, the chief mourner, Rena, asked Waka, one of her mother's Japanese friends with whom she felt at ease, to help her perform unfamiliar but fitting traditional funeral rituals for her mother.

Sumiko, Rena's mother, had left Japan as a teenager. She passed on her culture to her daughter through food and gestures rather than detailed explanations. 'As I was growing up', Rena remembered, 'I was not always at ease with being half

Japanese. My mother was very discreet; she never pushed me.' When Sumiko died, Rena chose to honour her mother by performing three traditional Japanese rituals of care, assisted by Waka. Rena wet her mother's lips using chopsticks and a cotton ball, symbolically giving her a last sip of water. Then she washed Sumiko's body and finally sprinkled the room with a sprig of evergreen dipped in salt water. *'As I performed these traditional Japanese gestures for my mother in my own Western context,'* Rena observed, *'I felt overwhelming gratitude to her for that part of my heritage.'*

RESPECT FOR PEOPLE AND RELATIONSHIPS

Harmonious ritualization respects people (present and absent), their relationships and interrelationships. The best-known summary of respect is the Golden Rule, which, in essence, means 'do no harm to oneself or others'. As a general rule, avoid taking rituals from foreign cultures and copy-pasting them into a ceremony. Use precaution with any unfamiliar ritual. If you do use one, introduce it consciously and conscientiously. Due regard for the feelings, wishes, rights and traditions of others strengthens social bonds.

In the example described above, Rena's use of the Japanese funeral rituals expressed her respect for her mother, their relationship and shared culture. Rena and Waka were respectful of the tradition. They did not confiscate or misuse rites from another culture, nor did they perform rituals that would usurp the role of a Shinto priest.

AESTHETICS SERVES NEED

'Aesthetics', a word derived from the Greek, refers to how we apprehend beauty through our senses, perception and feelings. Rituals are art-filled behaviours that transform everyday language, sounds and gestures in to something special. Any object introduced should be used during the ceremony.

At one funeral, there was a tall candle on a stand next to the coffin of a teenager who died in a motorcycle accident; it was never referred to or lit. In another ceremony, a memorial service for a young woman whose remains were buried abroad, the 10-year-old sister of the deceased wordlessly opened the ceremony carrying a lit tapered candle in both hands. The girl entered the ceremonial space to soft music, slowly making her way through a small labyrinth created by branches placed on the floor to the centre where a photo of her sister was propped up next to a tall candle on a stand. She paused before the photo, lit the tall candle, snuffed out her tapered candle, then made her way out of the labyrinth and took a seat next to her parents.

FORM FOLLOWS FUNCTION

'Form follows function', a main tenet of Bauhaus ideology, expresses the movement's reaction against design that hides the essence of an object under complex forms. In this context, the phrase is a reminder of the purpose of funerals: disposal of the body, leave-taking, support of mourners and peacefulness (see Chapter 2). Ritual profile determines ritual strategy, which affects the kind of funeral performed and also influences the choice of venue. When the assembly is aware of the reason for the choice, this knowledge can enhance sensemaking.

At the secular funeral of an architect who died by suicide, the presider welcomed the assembly, in the name of the man's family. Then he thanked the authorities for lending the church building for the ceremony. He briefly explained that building had been designed by the deceased who had considered it one of his best projects.

TRUTH TO MATERIALS

A carpenter uses a plumbline to true-up rough wood and works it until it is square, flat and smooth. Ritual craftspeople, like carpenters, must take time to true-up their materials. This begins with using the right person in the right place to say or do the right thing at the right time.

I gave in to family pressure at the funeral of a watchmaker and let the head of the man's professional association improvise his tribute. In his rambling 10-minute long monologue about the association, the man referred only once to his colleague. Not only did man's speech make the ceremony go over time, but everyone seemed embarrassed for the speaker. I later learned that the family had not dared to refuse the man's offer to say a word. If I had trued-up his text, the awkward situation could have been avoided.

SIMPLICITY: LESS IS MORE

Emotions tend to run high during a funeral ceremony. Complex concepts, sentences or ideas become difficult, if not impossible, to grasp. The Bauhaus-inspired brochure for Apple's first products proclaimed: 'Simplicity is the ultimate sophistication.'[4] The successful ritualmaker – whether beginner or advanced – uses a straightforward intuitive format, basic gestures and unpretentious everyday language. Communicate the heart of the ceremony (e.g. keywords) through repetition and short concise sentences in multiple art forms that appeal to the senses. The narrative of Sophia's funeral (Chapter 3) is an example of this a simple but elegant and meaningful funeral ceremony.

---

4   This quote is attributed to Leonardo da Vinci.

7

REALIZING THE CEREMONY

On Saturday, Gerry and Viviane's families, along with close friends, Dr Carole, the head nurse and the hospital pharmacist, gather in the cemetery where Audrey's great-grandparents are buried. Gerry and his brother carry Audrey's small coffin from the hearse to the gravesite. Hospital clowns playing a sad tune on plastic instruments follow them. Susan, the celebrant, opens the ceremonial moment and pronounces Audrey's full name, her date and place of birth and death. After a short silence, she reminds everyone of the memorial service the next day. At her signal, the clowns accompany the lowering of the casket with a melody chosen by Gabriela; heart-shaped messages of love flutter into the grave. Gerry and his brother take shovels and toss in a bit of dirt. It begins to drizzle as the mourners leave the ceremonial space. Aaron shouts, 'Sky sad too!'

The next afternoon, at one o'clock, Viviane, Gerry and their friends meet up with the care team at the hospital cafeteria. Tables are pushed aside and chairs placed in a semicircle before a blank wall that doubles as a background for the speakers and a screen for projected images. A large photo of Audrey, surrounded by her favourite toys, books and flowers, is hung at child's height. A low table is transformed into a miniature dandelion meadow. Stands for children's activities are decorated in the garden.

At two o'clock, a children's choir gathers and begins warming up. Half an hour later, Gabriela, Aaron and her cousins arrive with their grandparents and parents. The children walk up to Audrey's photo, chat softly and touch some of her toys. Finally, everything is ready. The family take their seats in the first row; care team members sit in the second row. Hospital security personnel stand near the doors ready to usher in mourners at the appointed time.

At three o'clock, the doors of the cafeteria open. The choir sings a cheerful but quiet piece as the mourners enter filling the room. Many wear white uniforms. Susan greets them all and thanks the hospital on the family's behalf for the use of the cafeteria. She explains briefly what to expect, then takes a dandelion clock and hands it to Gerry and Viviane. The parents express their hopes and dreams for their children, evoke the main events of Audrey's short life, and then blow together on the dandelion clock (see Figure 7.1).

Andy, Audrey's uncle, recalls that the twins were like little flower buds when they were first born. Audrey, whose favourite colour was yellow, opened like a sunny dandelion flower that faded too quickly. He picks a dandelion. Before blowing on it, he says that the flower will always remind him of the seeds of love Audrey planted in the family's heart.

Dr Carole talks about Audrey's bright smile but also the pain in her eyes and how hard it is to see someone you love suffer. Participating in the funeral, she adds, helps the care team assume their roles as healers – and as human beings. As she waves a dandelion clock, sunlight sparkles on a few white tufts.

Beth, a family friend, demonstrates a buzzing sound that Audrey made to distract herself from pain and boredom. She notes that missing Audrey feels like pain and invites everyone to make the buzzing sound with her: 'You can "buzz" whenever you miss Audrey.' Beth 'buzzes' on a dandelion clock to scatter the seeds.

'Every life – just like those dandelions – has a beginning, a middle and an end. When a life is over, it is complete,' observes Susan. 'Loss hurts, but it is not a contagious illness. Please don't avoid the family; they need your support.'

The ceremony closes with the choir's final song and the projection of photos of Audrey and her family. The clowns appear playing their plastic instruments and motioning to the children to follow them, first to a table laden with lemonade, muffins and cupcakes, then to the garden, where there are provisions for face painting and drawing as well as space to run about and play games.

Figure 7.1. Blowing on a dandelion clock
Although often cursed as a weed, the dandelion[1] is a nutritious plant that has been
gathered for food since prehistory. It is still used as a herbal remedy in Europe, North
America and China to treat infections, bile and liver problems, and as a diuretic. The
hardy plant thrives in difficult conditions. Yellow flower heads pepper fallow fields and
pop up through tiny cracks in the pavement. Since medieval times the dandelion has
symbolized the ability to push up against adversity, float above life's challenges and
initiate new life.

Why do we embark on the intensely creative and time-consuming
adventure of crafting and performing custom funeral ceremonies? Our
human need to explore, make sense of and mark the important events
in life is not entirely satisfied by planning and imagination. The creative
process requires a final step: taking action. Author Rita Mae Brown
believes 'we often disguise pain through ritual and it may be the only
solace we have' (1988, n.p.). As we saw in earlier chapters, people are

---

1   The plant's common name is derived from the French *dent-de-lion* (lion's tooth),
     which refers to the jagged shape of the plant's leaves. Its botanical name is *Taraxacum
     officinale*.

moved to do something that can transform or influence emotions or the outcome of a situation over which they have no control. Violent, sudden or accidental deaths, in particular, call for public actions of leave-taking which may be expressed through official or unofficial ceremonial words and gestures (see Figure 7.2).

Figure 7.2. RIP. When a life is over it is complete
'Just as a drop of water contains the entire ocean, a brief life span, with its rapid beginning, ephemeral zenith and fleeting end, is as meaningful as a long one. You just have to stoop a little to admire it, and come in close to tell its story.' (Chandernagor 2002; translation from the French by J. Gordon-Lennox)

LET THE MOURNERS ENTER

Decisions about funerals basically fall into two categories: reversible or irreversible. Not thanking all of the the people who sent you their condolences falls into the first category. If they are close friends you can thank them in person. The irreversible involves choices like whether or not to hold a public funeral or organizing a ceremony that failed to reflect the personality and values of the deceased. What happens when a funeral does not feel right? Isabel Russo, Head of Ceremonies at the British Humanist Association, says:

> I have heard innumerable accounts from people who attended 'traditional' religious funerals that left them alienated, frustrated and depressed because the platitudes offered were at best, irrelevant and at worst, an offensive contradiction to the values held by the person who had died. The complex process of recognition, acknowledgement and letting go of the deceased cannot take place at this type of funeral, and so the grieving process and subsequent healing process are stymied. Ritual is born of a deep need to articulate times of profound experience and transition, and that it is an essential part of what makes – and keeps – us human. Ritual that reflects the subject's belief system and the core elements that have meaning for them – makes for a psychologically healthier individual and by extension, for a substantially healthier society. (Russo 2017, pp.12–13)

The same frustration felt at conventional funerals may also arise during DIY funerals (see Ronald Grimes in Chapter 6). Although many of my colleagues and I have 'redone' inadequate funerals, years of pain and sorrow may go by before a more fitting memorial is performed.

SEPARATION, SUPPORT AND SERENITY

Some years ago, I observed that, no matter how untimely or terrible the death, a funeral that keeps the deceased at the centre lets mourners put the life of their loved one in perspective. Carla wrote: 'My husband's life celebration was held six months after his passing, followed by a 5k race for charity the next day. This life-affirming combo truly spoke to his unconventional self...laughter thru some tears and then a brisk run!'

Something happens as the chief mourners, surrounded by family and friends in a safe, supportive context, hear words and perform simple gestures that make sense while they experience the pain of separation. An homage that recounts the main events of the person's life and tributes that elaborate on their relationships put the bereaved on the same page. Feelings of sadness alternate with relief, and the sense of absence with a certain serenity. Everyone knows what the others know. The life of the deceased – however short – can be perceived as complete. The assembly as a whole shows signs of physical release. It is the ceremony, not the death certificate, that signals the radical change from life to death – and initiates a new relationship between the living and the dead.

Dissanayake: How does ritual practice help us?

Art-filled ritual practices address and satisfy evolved needs of human psychology. They create and reinforce emotionally reassuring and psychologically necessary feelings of close relationship with others and of belonging to a group. Further, they provide to individuals a sense of meaningfulness or cognitive order and individual competence insofar as they give emotional force to explanations of how the world came to be as it is and what is required to maintain it. They are adaptive not only because they join people together in common cause but because they also relieve anxiety. It is better to have something to do, with others, in times of uncertainty rather than try to cope by oneself or do nothing at all. (Dissanayake, personal communication 2016)

ALONE WE MAY GO FASTER, TOGETHER WE GO FURTHER

The collective experience of a personalized public ceremony – even when it involves only a few simple words and acts at a gravesite or during the dispersal of ashes – lends a sense of cohesion to an often disparate group.

These ceremonial moments offer comfort, and inaugurate a new reality within which the participants can evolve, individually and collectively, in peace. It is an opportunity to gradually and gently weave new meaning – no matter how bittersweet – into the fabric of daily life. This remarkable interplay between the individual and the group can transform people and foster an organic communal body that enhances social, and even geopolitical, stability.

REALIZING PHASE

This phase is broken down into three parts: preparation time (variable), ceremony (5 to 50 minutes) and social gathering (2 to 4 hours).

RISK FACTORS FOR THE REALIZING PHASE

Avoid adding last-minute stress to an already emotional occasion by having speakers arrive at the funeral venue prepared and at least 30 minutes early. If a sound system is used, each speaker should test the microphone with their own voice well before the assembly arrives. Avoid complex ideas and acts and keep the ceremony short. Remember that the attention span of mourners is limited. The presider is solely responsible for carrying the ceremony and respecting the time frame. This includes making sure water and a few cups are available for anyone who feels faint. Especially in hot weather, the participants may appreciate being greeted with water or fruit juice. Reserve alcoholic drinks for the social gathering.

> **Behind the scenes...**
> The evening after Audrey's funeral, Gerry calls everyone to him saying: 'Family hug!' He puts one arm around Viviane who is holding Aaron, catches up Gabriela with the other arm and whispers: 'We won't forget about you, ever, darling Audrey.' Viviane nods and adds: 'She would have enjoyed her funeral... Now I feel like we could go back to that hospital if Gabriela or Aaron ever need care.'

TOOLBOX

TOOLS FOR THE REALIZING PHASE

The two tools presented here guide family and friends as they prepare for the last phase of the funeral ceremony.

Guidelines for readers

Readers should arrive prepared for public speaking (appearance, text and voice). In highly emotional situations like a funeral, it is a good idea to place someone in the audience where they can be a comforting presence or to have that person accompany you to the lectern. Do not hesitate to arrange for a backup person to take over – just in case you really cannot get through the tribute. When such provisions are made, people may still find they need to stop to catch their breath or wipe away a tear, but they rarely need the backup.

- Your role is important but secondary to the occasion.
- If you are reading a text of your own composition, submit it well in advance to those crafting the ritual.
- Practise reading aloud.
- Stand rather than sit: it is easier to feel grounded and remain attentive to your feelings.
- Test your voice – with the microphone – well before people arrive. When using a handheld microphone, press it lightly against your chin and hold it there throughout the reading; it will follow the movements of your head and project your voice evenly.
- Walk up to the lectern at a natural pace. Exhale as slowly as you can. Place your feet slightly apart. Do not lock your knees. Inhale lightly. Begin reading, very very slowly.
- Keep hand and facial gestures to a minimum. Link your hands behind your back or let them fall comfortably at your side. Do not put them in your pockets or grip or lean over the lectern.
- If emotions do well up, let them. Pause. Drink some water. Exhale slowly; inhale. If you still feel like you cannot carry on, move to the side of the lectern, and signal your backup person to take over.

Preparing the setting

Setting up for a graveside ceremony usually begins about half an hour beforehand. In the case of a funeral like the one held at the hospital for Audrey, count on two hours of preparation. The sound system team, decorators, florists and caterer (if reception is held in the same room) should be in place and ready at least an hour before the announced time and the arrival of the assembly.

At this point, the people actively involved in the ceremony (presider, craftspeople, greeters, participants, musicians) are present. Those using a microphone should test it. If the reception area is within earshot of the ceremonial space, the caterers must keep quiet or take a break during the ceremony; they must be ready to serve, however, the minute it is over.

Opening and carrying the event

When the presider indicates it is time to begin, the greeters may show the guests to their seats. A change in the music – or a short silence if music is already being played – signals an entrance or a transition in the ceremony. The presider also deals with unexpected events such as late arrivals, crying children, noise from passing vehicles or a person who is unwell. This may mean modifying the procedure, shifting everyone's attention away or, on the contrary, simply stating what is happening.

Transitioning from ceremony to socializing

The presider should preserve a solemn tone as she or he closes the ceremony. Explanations about when and how to leave the ceremonial space are given only if they are absolutely necessary. The assembly usually readily follows the chief mourners' lead. The role of an organizer is to ensure that there are no obstacles to people moving smoothly from the formal ceremonial space to where the social gathering is held.

Closing the event

At the end of the funeral reception, the organizer is attentive to people's needs as they make ready to leave. She or he assumes responsibility for or supervises the clean-up.

NOTES ON FUNERALS FOR SENSITIVE SITUATIONS

Have you ever wondered if you are insensitive because you were not devastated by the death of someone really close to you? Or, perhaps you worry that you are oversensitive because you were unexpectedly hard hit by the loss of an acquaintance or a pet? Different factors affect our sense of loss, such as our identification with the deceased, special ties and unfinished business, but also timing, cause and circumstances of death.

The losses that we dread the most or that touch us deeply are not necessarily the most problematic when it comes to arranging a funeral. Once again, the choice of funeral rituals is determined by ritual profile and strategy (Chapter 2). The same goes for all commemorative practices.[2] Most cultural traditions mark death with a ceremony. How they circumscribe bereavement often depends on the mourner's relationship to the dead and the cause of death.

Although we may not feel the need to wear black, cover our mirrors or purify ourselves after the death of a loved one, delimiting mourning in time and space is beneficial, particularly in the case of sensitive situations. We can introduce a sense of time in mourning by doing something special on significant dates (birthday, anniversary of death) or by marking the seasons since the funeral. The ordinary is made extraordinary by performing practical acts with intentionality (ordering and placing a tombstone on the grave or spreading the ashes). Not only do such ceremonial moments and commemorative acts meet our human need to contain grief but they lessen

---

2   'Commemorate' is a communal call to be mindful of relationships. It comes from the late sixteenth-century Latin word commemorat- 'brought to remembrance', which is composed of the verb commemorare, from com- 'altogether' + memorare 'relate' (from memor 'mindful').

the sense of isolation by strengthening social ties that keep mourners in the flow of life.

PARENT, PARENT-FIGURE OR GUARDIAN

The demise of a parent removes a protective generational barrier between the child and death. A young child who loses a parent is often marked for life. An adult child too may be emotionally unprepared for this loss, even in the case of aged parents or long-term illness. Parents who leave their material or emotional affairs in disorder compound any sense of abandonment, betrayal and loss their child may have. When cultural prescriptions for mourning a parent are inadequate or lacking, children can introduce specific times for mourning and acts of remembrance.

SPOUSE OR PARTNER

Nothing disrupts daily life as much as the death of a spouse or a partner. At first, the survivor may appear to be the strongest person in the couple's entourage. Some insist on assuming funeral arrangements single-handedly. As chief mourners they may want to express their feelings during the funeral but do not trust their voice. Alternatives include performing a significant gesture, sitting in a prominent place or asking the celebrant to lend them her or his voice and read their message for them. The survivor may find it difficult to delimit mourning in time and space. Unlike the other mourners who can return to their routines, the survivor often finds her or himself navigating the currents of life without an anchor and familiar landmarks. Isolation can hit like a full-force gale. For this reason, partners should avoid major changes such as moving house, marrying or taking on a new job during the first year.

CHILDREN, TEENAGERS AND YOUNG ADULTS

A woman who loses her partner to death is known as a widow,

a man who loses his is a widower. A child bereft of parents is an orphan. But English does not have a name for parents who lose a child before or after birth. It seems so unacceptable, so out of the order of things, for children to die before their parents. Regardless of the cause of death, bereaved parents may feel guilty about their utter helplessness to protect or save their child. They tend to report more depressive symptoms, poorer wellbeing, and more health problems than parents who have never lost a child.

Parents grieve loss differently. Separation and divorce is frequent among bereaved parents. The couple's relationship fares better when they adopt a common ritual strategy for the funeral and nourish their relationship with ceremonial moments that contain their grief in time and space.

CHILDREN AND DEATH

A child who is old enough to love is old enough to grieve and mourn the loss of a loved one. Speak with children using clear language[3] that is adapted to their age and their perception of death. This will help them understand that (1) the person will not return, (2) the death is not their fault and (3) they are not responsible for 'fixing' the sadness around them. Adults do not need to hide their grief from children but they are encouraged to express it in an environment that feels safe and secure to the child.

Children and teenagers should be invited, but not forced, to

---

3   Avoid euphemisms when speaking about death. This is particularly important when telling young children and even teens about the death of a loved one or a pet. Phrases such as 'Aunt Doris left us', 'Doug lost his life in a train accident', 'Grandma passed away/went to a better place', 'Spot was put to sleep', 'Daddy's gone to heaven/to be with Jesus', 'baby Jeannie slipped away from us', 'Lucy didn't make it' and 'we lost uncle Freddy' are more frightening than straight talk. In the same way, news that a child's father is 'very sick' or 'getting ready to die soon', are preferable to 'not doing very well' or 'going home'. Euphemisms are not only confusing but they may conjure up images about illness and death that result in nightmares and unrealistic fears about travel, minor illness, nodding off to sleep or anaesthesia during medical interventions.

attend and even participate in the funeral. Lending a hand with the creation of rituals may help them channel their emotion. It is important that an adult with whom the child or teen feels safe – if possible someone less affected by the death – accompany her or him on the day of the funeral. The illness of a parent should not be hidden from a child. The death of a family pet or a favourite plant should be dealt with in a similar manner. When handled with honesty and tact, these 'lesser losses' prepare children to face adversity and live life more fully.

SUDDEN OR VIOLENT DEATH

The shock of death is that much greater when it occurs suddenly or as a result of violence. Death by accidental fire or disaster, drowning, cot death, a traffic, rail, aircraft or climbing accident, indiscriminate assault or crime, suicide or death in the context of political unrest, armed conflict or war are particularly devastating for survivors.

How authorities, public services and the press handle the situation is crucial, especially when a death is due to technical or human failure. As often as not, survivors suddenly find themselves exposed to the harsh critical light of public curiosity. Timely information, explanations, apologies and condolences as well as assistance in repatriating the body can ease feelings of horror and injustice. Public funerals for multiple deaths should be secular in tone, presided by a secular representative in a non-religious setting – unless all of the victims practised the same religion. Civil authorities should make provisions for ephemeral rituals to remember the dead in public spaces.

SUICIDE

In the past, people who died by suicide were rarely entitled to a funeral or even a proper burial, perhaps because of the active role they took in their death. This may also be the case for elderly or ill people who chose to terminate their suffering.

Although the stigma of these choices remains in many places, compassion for survivors should prevail over moral judgement. As is the case for any accidental or violent death, mourners need the support of a public funeral, which should always include a brief explanation for the untimely death. References to suicide or voluntary death must be carefully formulated and validated by the chief mourners.

ABSENT BODY AND FORCED DISAPPEARANCE

In conventional mourning, time eventually blurs memories and chips away at the sharpest edges of grief. When death occurs far from home and the body cannot be found or repatriated – as in the case of a mountain expedition, an avalanche or an aircraft or boating accident – it may make the evening news and the dead may have a proper funeral. But, even years after the event, it can still feel unreal to survivors who may find themselves scanning passers-by on the street in search of their loved one's face.

Dealing with forced disappearance in a context of political unrest and war is even more pernicious. Where there is neither a body, nor any proof or even reliable information about a death, the past is never truly past. Absence tortures memory and freezes the grief of chief mourners who have no public support or official status (widow, widower, orphan). In such cases, an act of social protest or a ceremonial moment in a context that strongly evokes intimate memories for survivors can 'certify absence' (but never death). This event may suffice to chisel a 'before' and an 'after' in time and memory, thus freeing family and friends to integrate the reality of the loss in their daily lives. And, most importantly, resist the deliberate torture inherent to the practice of forced disappearance.

PART IV

THE FUTURE OF THE DEAD

The earlier parts of this guide consider mortality – our own
and that of those we love — present an updated view of
ritual and offer guidance and practical tools for planning,
creating and performing meaningful funeral rituals. The book
closes with a brief look at the future of the dead. In particular,
it explores how art-filled public commemoration events
enhance bonds between the living and the dead.

8

NEW MOURNING

As Mikkel arrives at the Silkeborg cemetery (Denmark) to tend to his family gravesite, he spots Dorthe, a local shopkeeper, cleaning up the grave of a young child. Recognizing him as a client, she nods and raises her coffee thermos in greeting. She asks him if he's heard about the public event to honour the dead that will take place that afternoon at the graveyard. Mikkel says he's intrigued, and a bit wary. They agree to return later to see what it's about.

At four o'clock Mikkel picks out Dorthe in the group gathered around glowing firepits at the cemetery gates. She steps towards him, 'I have never seen so much activity at the graveyard!' Volunteers greet newcomers and direct them to different stations set up throughout the cemetery grounds. A leaf carpet crackles under visitors' feet as they diffidently walk towards the first station. Under a tree decorated with a dozen storylines,[1] a smiling cemetery employee supervises bulb planting and encourages visitors to return in the spring to see the new life push up through the snow.

Upended logs with blankets, arranged artfully around a firepit, invite people to take it slowly, and even sit for a spell. Dorthe and Mikkel wander among the headstones until they come to the second station where the Goose Game awaits them (see Figure 8.2).[2] Mikkel picks up a plump goose piece that reminds him of his sister Anni's good humour. On the first round, he places it on the image of a tree and mentions that his sister loved to walk in the forest. The second time around, Mikkel throws the dice and comes up with

---

1 These storylines represent shorter and longer lives. They are composed of crumpled pages from old books that had been strung together, like popcorn, and hung from the branches of the tree. All of the ritual concepts performed at Silkeborg are copyrighted by Ida van der Lee.

2 The Goose Game is a board game that is thought to have originated in sixteenth-century Europe. The Goose Game created by van der Lee is a large cloth with a spiral track composed of 63 images.

a five. Moving his piece five spaces forward would put it on a skull; if he sends it backward it will land on an acorn. Mikkel chooses the skull and recounts in a soft voice that Anni, who was often depressed, had died by suicide. 'She left a note, but I've felt so guilty. I wish she'd chosen new life (acorn) instead of death (skull),' Mikkel says. 'I guess I couldn't have stopped her.'

The next station is laid out with Memory Things (see Figure 8.1). Mikkel selects a tiny book and places it in a niche with a candle and a note for his sister. Some people quietly share their experiences with a volunteer. Mikkel sits on a stump near a firepit and enfolds himself in a blanket and companionable silence while Dorthe moves on to Melting Frozen Pain. She picks up a small flat stick, writes 'anger' on it and nudges it carefully into the flames of the firepit. An attentive volunteer hands Dorthe an ice cube containing rosehip seeds; she slips it in the pot hanging above the fire. While waiting for the ice to melt, she imagines the pain of her anger disappearing with the cube. After a time, Dorthe is aware that Mikkel is standing nearby.

They stop at the Dining with the Dead station for coffee or tea served in porcelain cups at a beautifully dressed table. Conversations naturally turn to what it means to lose a loved one. Laughter mingles with tears. Dorthe admits that her marriage did not survive the loss of their child. Mikkel reveals that he is emerging from a painful divorce; he adds that he'd never imagined that silence could feel so supportive. As the sky darkens, they stop to admire handmade lanterns. A cemetery employee at the back gate wishes them 'Go'aften' (Good evening)!

MARKING THE TRANSITION TO A NEW STATUS

What happens to the dead after they are dead? Imagining the future of the dead evokes a contradiction in terms, particularly in the context of Western culture with its linear view of time. Can the dead be a part of our future? In a world of rapid social and technological change where the health of the planet is a priority[3] and 'perpetuity' now means 10- or 30-year-long leases on gravesites, current interest in the 'afterdeath' reflects practical issues rather than metaphysical concerns.

Figure 8.1. Niches for memories

'My grandmother's ashes are in an unmarked grave,' Malou explained. 'The only time I went there I called out: "Where are you, Grandma?" So, two years ago, when my husband Karl found out he was terminally ill and told us just to put him in a cardboard box and drop him off at the landfill, I protested. Karl finally agreed to a proper grave when he saw how much it meant to us. My sons and I come here all the time to chat to him. It was good to remember him today and experience this event together.'

© J. Gordon-Lennox

The dead have two lives, explained sociologist Robert Hertz in a paper

---

3   Lifelong recyclers, for example, want no embalming, and biodegradable solutions for disposal and green cemeteries that look like parks where one can picnic with the family.

written in 1907: one in nature, as matter, and one in culture, as social beings. Until recently, Hertz observes, our mourning for the dead relied on rituals that dealt with them as matter. An unwritten agreement between next of kin, the undertaker and the religious leader held that the dead would be treated with dignity and that the family would not ask about alternatives to the conventional funeral such as traditional liturgical practices, embalming, the costly coffin, grave plot and headstone (Economist 2018). Today, the future dead preplan and the bereaved ask questions about the options.[4] The increase in direct disposals and cremations leaves us less matter to deal with and turns the conventional funeral model on its head.

At the same time, our sense of the dead as social beings grows, along with a certain dissatisfaction with the range of memorial forms currently available to us. The need for ceremony and ritual has never been so great. Societies like Japan and India,[5] where cremation is nearly universal, base mourning on ritual practices that enhance the ongoing social life of the dead. Funeral rituals extend well beyond the time frame allotted to Western mourners. Personal ritual practices such as maintaining a corner of a shelf with mementos of the dead, and public ritual gestures like incense-burning, link the seeking, creating and taking of meaning to a continuous memorial process.

---

4   Americans each year bury 70,000 cubic metres of hardwood, enough to build 2000 single-family houses. They use 1.6m tonnes of reinforced concrete for vaults. Cremation is gaining popularity in part because it seems less wasteful. Burning (ever larger) bodies uses resources too. A conventional gas-fired crematorium blasts 320kg of carbon into the atmosphere per body (the equivalent of a 20-hour car journey) and 2 to 4 grams of mercury from teeth fillings. In 1960, only 4 per cent of Americans were cremated; this is expected to rise to 79 per cent by 2035. Cremation rose in China from 33 per cent in 1995 to 50 per cent in 2012. In Japan, where the practice is seen as purification for the next life, it is nearly universal (Economist 2018).

5   Primal (original) or local religions and cultures, with their spirit worlds and more horizontal – or at least less global – social structures, quite naturally integrate the social aspect, or spirit, of the dead in public and private ritual practice.

Figure 8.2. Geese always find their way!
At the Goose Game station, anthropologist Nina Faartoft (left), a celebrant trainer at
the Danish Humanist Society, invites Rie and her sister Christina to choose a goose
figure that reminds them of their mother. Rie selects a sturdy goose, 'My mother was
a very down-to-earth kind of person.' She places the figure on the image of a cat and
says, 'Mum had a cat she really appreciated, especially in the last days.' Christina throws
a dice and places her goose on the drawing of an inventor's machine and says, 'I sure
hope that one day there will be a cure for the bloody cancer that killed our mother.'

© *J. Gordon-Lennox*

As commemoration of the dead evokes the primary sense of the
word, mindfulness together, emerging ritual practices aim for lasting
social relationships between the bereaved and the deceased. Acts of
memorialization are fundamentally social rituals built with basic ritual
materials: *people, participation* and physical and virtual *place*. They are
often structured around important dates, and make use of personal
objects that have special significance for the bereaved. Alternative public
rituals include: dedicated objects like gravestones or park benches; events
such as memorial services; ongoing activities, like memorial foundations;

and the use of new technologies through the creation of online memorials (Corpse Project 2018; Remember Me 2018).

COMMEMORATION FOR THE DEAD: CEMETERY IN SILKEBORG, DENMARK

The day of the dead commemoration, described in the narrative above, is an example of a successful public memorialization of the dead. The event, which took place in 2018, was the first of its kind in Denmark. It is not an offshoot of contemporary Halloween or Mexican Day of the Dead events. No one wore masks or costumes, performed tricks, handed out candy treats or jumped out and cried: Boo! The commemoration was characterized by a warm welcome, the simple beauty of a natural lakeside setting, carefully thought-out activities and attentive accompaniment.

Ritual artist Ida van der Lee invented the concept in 2005 for a cemetery near her home.[6] Since then, each year on an evening in early November, cemeteries throughout the Netherlands sponsor similar memorial events. Spontaneity and improvisation are not on the agenda. Van der Lee trained local Danish volunteers over a three-month period for this commemoration of the dead.[7] On the day of the event, 45 volunteers accompanied several hundred visitors of all ages as they freely wandered through the cemetery (see Figures 8.1 and 8.2). In 2019, a similar commemoration took place in a cemetery in Copenhagen.

The Dutch and the Danish are not the only ones creating new occasions for participative public remembrance.

---

6   See Ida van der Lee's personal website (2019) for detailed descriptions and other examples of her work.

7   Dutch curator Anne Berk suggested that Iben From, the director of the Silkeborg Bad KunstCentret, invite ritual artist Ida van der Lee to organize this commemoration as a complement to her exhibition entitled 'Beyond the Body'. The enthusiasm of the director of the Silkeborg cemetery made it happen. Local volunteers were coordinated by KK44, a cultural church group.

185 CHAIRS: EARTHQUAKE SITE IN CHRISTCHURCH, NEW ZEALAND

On the day of the first memorial service to the 2011 earthquake victims at Christchurch, local artist Peter Majendie arranged 185 empty chairs that he had painted white on the site of a demolished church. Like the victims, each chair in the installation has its own distinct personality. There are armchairs, dining room chairs, a wheelchair and even a baby capsule. Majendie invites visitors to select a chair to sit in and reflect. The poetic arrangement, intended by the artist as a short-term installation (1–3 weeks) and a reminder of the ephemerality of life, has become a major tourist attraction (see Figure 8.3).

Figure 8.3. 185 empty chairs
'A temporary art installation reflecting on the loss of lives, livelihood and living in our city following the earthquake on 22 February 2011. You are welcome to spend time in this place.' This message greets visitors at the site of the installation by artist Peter Majendie. The 185 empty chairs honour the 185 victims of the 2011 Christchurch earthquake and give the survivors an opportunity to sit among them.

DE TU PUÑO Y LETRA (BY YOUR OWN HAND): BULLRING IN QUITO, ECUADOR

In Ecuador, an estimated 6 out of every 10 women are victims of violent acts, too many of which are fatal; only 10 per cent escape their violent partners. In 2014 artist Suzanne Lacy used art to create a space for a public

Figure 8.4. 10,000 handwritten letters
When artist Suzanne Lacy arrived in Quito, she was introduced to the archive Cartas de Mujeres, which contains 10,000 handwritten letters by women. As she read some of them, Lacy realized that the project wasn't finished yet and asked: Could we create a public response to the letters through art? Lacy then began asking questions with participants about what might be possible. Scores of collaborators, including male participants, worked together to challenge perceptions of masculinity and domestic violence.

response to domestic violence (see Figure 8.4). After a careful analysis of the local environment, Lacy identified two objectives: first, publicly respond to the women's suffering and unanswered pleas for action. Second, include men more centrally in the issue of domestic violence.

The result was a live performance in a bullring in Quito where men read the women's letters about their childhood, their body, and intimate partner violence.[8] As the bullring slowly filled with 300 men of all ages and from all walks of life (including many police officers), their voices rose in a crescendo of sound that was abruptly broken by silence. An elderly white-haired woman standing among the men, asked: 'Why do you call this love?'

Surprise interventions from live musicians seated in the audience added to the theatricality and poignancy of the performance and paved the way for the last act. Scattered among the spectators, the 300 men huddled over candles to read 'their' letters to intimate groups of two or three people. The audience exploded into conversation as people sat with open hearts listening and responding to each other, with more than a few tears. Formerly hidden experiences were transformed by the full light of an inclusive public conversation that, hopefully, continued long after the end of the performance.

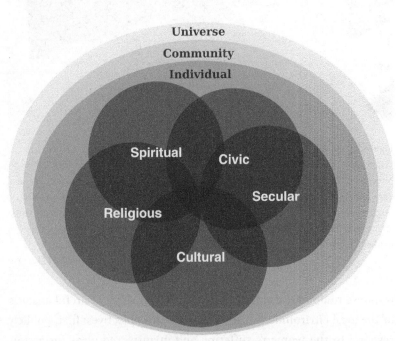

Figure 8.5. Scope of memorial rituals
Scope of memorial rituals is broad and may cover one or several areas (secular, spiritual, religious, civic and cultural). They have an impact on individuals, communities and beyond.

---

8   See Suzanne Lacy's personal website (2019) for a video and photos of the performance.

MEMORIAL RITUALS IN PUBLIC SPACES[9]

Public memorials may elicit responses that change how we see our own lives and even the world (see Figure 8.5). The three memorializations described in this chapter are remarkable for their apparent simplicity and socio-cultural dimension, as well as their private and public impact. They create a space that is artistic, but not art; events that are theatrical, not theatre; therapeutic, not therapy; voluntary, not imposed; celebratory, but not a party; playful, but not a game. By offering a time-out-of-time – not a traumatizing time-out – for interaction and reflection, these participative memorial events allow us to come to grips with what it means to be human and to survive. All three use different ways and means to support ongoing management of the relationship between life and death, victims and survivors, the living and the dead.

The artists repackage ritual using the three phases of the creative process: planning, creating, realizing (see Figure 6.1 in Chapter 6). The six rules for ritualmaking apply as they create meaning in a way that makes sense to active and passive participants (see Figure 6.1 and *Notes on rules for ritual design* in Chapter 6). The six pillars of the craft guide participants and visitors as they seek and take meaning: need, content, roles, context, sensemaking, coherence (see *Notes on the pillars of ritual design* in Chapter 5).

The significance of these new memorial practices in an increasingly secular society is ongoing. They provide a focus for social transition by considering our individual and collective biological need to do something, to feel safe and to contain strong emotion. Fitting communal multisensory activities, like these, help us mark time and space. They anchor us solidly in the present and our memories firmly in reality.

Ritual practices point us towards the future by helping us achieve intentionality (or power or energy) that is directed at objects and goals. This intentionality, which is both individual and collective, reinforces

---

9   New public memorial activity has generated new vocabulary, with words like deathscapes and consolationscapes.

physical, psychological, social and cultural links between the living and the dead (see Figure 8.5).

RISK FACTORS FOR PUBLIC MEMORIALIZATION

The main risks for public memorialization lie in creating work or events that miss the point. Meaningful memorials are about the future of the dead as social beings. As we saw in the three examples above, simplicity is the ultimate sophistication. Memorials that favour the aesthetic over meaning draw attention to the work itself rather than to the subject of the work. Incoherent and inauthentic public memorials can engender feelings of coldness, confusion and loneliness. Let's take up the challenge to assume the future of the dead by writing our own history. If we don't, we run the risk of having others – or the marketing industry – do it for us.

> **Behind the scenes...**
> Pliny the Younger considered writing a way to ensure the future of the dead. Neither he nor his story have been forgotten.[10]
>
> > Whether posterity will remember us I do not know. But we certainly deserve distinction. Not for our genius, for this would sound arrogant, but for our dedication, labor, and concern for the future. We will continue on the road that we have taken which, while it carries few into the full light of fame, leads many from the shadow of oblivion. (1900, *Letters* 9.XIV)
>
> In his correspondence with his friends, Pliny discusses loss and consolation.
>
> > Temper the serious with the joyous, lest the former should degenerate

---

10 The population in the danger zone around Vesuvius has risen to 3 million people. Real estate promoters and developers tell people that the volcano is extinct. Scientists, who detect magma building up in the chamber below the mountain, disagree (Hughes 2013, p.132).

into melancholy, and the latter run up into levity. With this plan in mind, I chose a convenient place and time...

If you should think it proper to write to him upon the [death of his daughter], let me remind you not to use the rougher arguments of consolation but those of kind and sympathizing humanity. (1900, *Letters* XCIV to Arrianus)

The truly human feel sorrow and want consolation. There is a certain pleasure even in giving vent to one's grief; especially when we weep on the bosom of a friend who will approve, or, at least, pardon, our tears. (1900, *Letters* XC to Paternus)

GLOSSARY

Terminology related to death and funerals is, fortunately, not something most of us need to use on a daily basis. Many of the words appear in this book, others are for general information.

Bereaved People who have recently lost an immediate family member or close friend. Mourner.

Casket Box-shaped item distinguished by its rectangular shape, sometimes confused with a coffin. The term also applies to an ornamental box or chest used for holding valuables.

Catafalque A wooden stand or metal support on which a coffin or casket is placed; it may be decorated or covered with a drape.

Cenotaph An empty tomb or monument in honour of a person whose remains are elsewhere.

Chapel of rest A room, usually in a funeral home, where the body may be viewed before the funeral.

Coffin A long, narrow box, typically of wood, in which a corpse is buried or cremated. Unlike a rectangular casket, a coffin is tapered at both ends.

Columbarium A niche for an urn that holds the ashes remaining after cremation. More commonly it refers to a room, a building or a wall with small compartments to store funeral urns.

Committal service A ceremony where the coffin, casket or funeral urn is buried. It can be part of or separate from the funeral ceremony or take place when the body is removed for cremation.

Coronach will A document detailing what kind of ceremony a person wants for their funeral and committal services. It may include instructions for the reception and where they want to be buried or have their ashes spread.

Coroner   An official who investigates violent, sudden or suspicious deaths, as well as cases where the dead is unidentified.

Cortege   A solemn procession. Traditionally, a procession of mourners travelling on foot behind the vehicle conveying the corpse in a casket or coffin – more rarely a funeral urn – from the venue where the funeral ceremony was held to the place of burial.

Death certificate   An official statement signed by a physician that states the cause, date and place of a person's death.

Death mask   A likeness of the dead person's face typically made by taking a cast or impression in wax or plaster directly from the corpse. When taken from a living subject, such a cast is called a *life* mask. A *funeral* mask is an image placed on the face of the deceased before burial rites, and normally buried with them (e.g. Tutankhamun's mask and the mask of Agamemnon).

Death wails   Traditionally, sounds, vocal lament or music announce, mourn or remember the dead. A few examples are the ringing of special bells, coronach, dirge, equale (or aequale, a trombone choir), keening, dirge and threnody (wailing ode, song, hymn or poem).

Disbursements   Costs paid by the funeral director on the behalf of the bereaved to third parties such as crematorium fees, flowers and venue hire.

Disposal of human corpses   The main methods for disposing of dead bodies today include biocremation, burial, cremation, excarnation, infinity burial, promession, sea burial, sky burial and space burial.

   Biocremation   A process that employs alkaline hydrolysis (using lye and heat) for the disposal of human corpses (also referred to as resomation, flameless cremation or water cremation). The remains can be disposed of as ashes or used as compost.

   Burial   One of the most common practices in Western society for disposing of a human corpse, also known as interment or inhumation. It involves excavating a pit or trench, placing a dead person or animal in it and filling it in with earth. Contrary to conventional ideas, only corpses carrying an infectious disease require immediate burial or cremation.[1] See also **Sea burial**.

Cremation   Among one of the most common practices today in Western society for disposing of a human corpse. It involves burning it to ashes on a funeral pyre or in a special oven. The remains, known as 'cremains', are commonly stored in an urn, or scattered on land or water.

Excarnation   A common practice for disposing of a cadaver, also known as defleshing, where the flesh is removed or left to decompose naturally over a certain period of time, leaving only the bones. Sky burial and *mos Teutonicus* are two forms of excarnation. The latter was practised by German Crusaders during the Middle Ages in order to repatriate the bodies of high status individuals. The practice was common in the production of relics that were kept for veneration.

Infinity burial suit   A recent process for the disposal of human or animal bodies that employs a biodegradable suit or shroud instead of a casket or coffin. The suit is composed of a biomix made up of mushrooms and other microorganisms that together do three things: aid in decomposition, work to neutralize toxins found in the body and transfer vital nutrients that enrich the earth and foster new life.

Body donation   The donation of a whole body after death for research and educational purposes. Some donation programmes have a communal grave dedicated to body donors, others may

---

1   Precipitous mass burials, incineration or collective disposal of cadavers is not only unnecessary but contrary to local socio-cultural practices and has serious consequences on mental health. The expedited mass disposal of victims commonly practised after a natural disaster or armed conflict is a result not of informed medical knowledge but of political pressure, says health advisor De Ville de Goyet. Identification of the body is essential to the grieving process. Mass burials inhibit mourning a close relative, leave lingering doubts on the whereabouts of the disappeared and condemn the surviving spouse or child to a legal limbo that exacerbates mental health problems. Survivors of a catastrophe are more likely than the dead to be a source of disease outbreak (De Ville de Goyet 2004).

cover the cost of cremation or burial and return the body to the family for interment. Also referred to as giving one's body to science, anatomical donation or body bequest. See also **Organ donation**.

Promession   A process for disposal of a human body developed by Swedish biologist Susanne Wiigh-Mäsak in 1997 that involves cryogenic freezing with liquid nitrogen. After freeze-drying, the remains are sifted to remove any metal pieces and then placed in a biodegradable casket which, once interred, decomposes into humus in as little as 6–12 months. The company was dissolved in 2015 for lack of funds for the construction of a facility.

Sea burial   The disposal of human remains in the ocean, normally from a ship or boat. It is regularly performed by navies, and is done by private citizens in many countries.

Sky burial   A practice for disposing of a human corpse, also known as excarnation, in which it is placed near a mountain top, on a platform or at the top of a tower to decompose naturally or be eaten by scavenging animals. Examples are Tibetan sky burial, Comanche platform burials and traditional Zoroastrian towers of silence. Numerous solar concentrators recently installed in Mumbai palliate the shortage of vultures (due to use of toxic medications in humans and animals). The concentrators turn the cadaver to bone in just three days.

Space burial   The practice of launching cremains into space.

DIY funeral   The distinction of a do-it-yourself (DIY) funeral is its organization by the chief mourners rather than by funeral professionals.

Embalming   A technique used to preserve a corpse from decay. Traditionally, dead bodies were preserved with spices; now it is usually done by arterial injection of chemical preservatives.

Epitaph   A phrase or statement written in memory of a person who has died, especially as an inscription on a tombstone.

Executor   Someone named in a will to be responsible for the management of an estate, usually a close friend or family member of the person who has passed away.

Exhume   The act of removing remains from a burial site, sometimes for investigation or identification, usually for reburial elsewhere. Most countries require a licence for exhumation.

Funeral celebrant   A non-religious professional who leads the funeral ceremony. This person may pronounce a eulogy or invite others to do so. In some cases this refers to religious personnel.

Funeral director   A professional, also known as an undertaker, whose business is to manage funerals, burials and cremations.

Funeral parlour   An establishment, also called a funeral home, where the dead are prepared for burial or cremation.

Funerary art   Any work of art forming, or placed in, a repository for the remains of the dead. The term encompasses a wide variety of forms, including prehistoric megalithic constructs, cenotaphs and war memorials.

Hearse/first call coach   A vehicle specially designed to carry a coffin or casket.

Homage   Special honour or respect shown publicly. Traditionally, doing homage was a formal public acknowledgement of feudal allegiance. In this context it denotes the central feature of the ceremony in that it provides an overview of the life and work of the deceased. Doing homage may take forms: words (elegy, encomium, eulogy, panegyric); music (requiem, threnody); dance; theatrical piece; art (painting, sculpture). See also **Tribute**.

Humanist funeral   A funeral based on humanist philosophy. The ceremony, usually lead by a humanist celebrant, focuses on the life and personality of the person who has died rather than on religious rites and notions about what might happen after death.

Green burial   Also known as eco-friendly funeral, woodland burial or natural burial. A funeral that strives to be as environmentally friendly as possible, usually involving a compostable casket or urn and disposal in a natural setting.

Lair (Scottish)   A word that designates a burial plot or grave.

Living will   A document detailing how someone wants to be cared for if they cannot make their wishes known because they lack consciousness or agency in the later stages of their life.

Mausoleum   A kind of above-ground edifice with several tombs for permanent storage of a corpse (also referred to as immurement).

Medical certificate of cause of death   A certificate issued by a doctor confirming how a person died. In some places this document is needed to get a death certificate.

Memorial ceremony   Similar to a funeral service, the memorial ceremony is usually conducted in the absence of the body.

Mortician   A person who prepares the body for burial or cremation using certain procedures or gestures such as embalming, makeup, reconstruction and dressing the dead. Also known as a mortuary technician.

Necrology   A register or list of records of the deaths of people related to a particular organization, family, group or field of interest.

Obituary   A notice of a death, especially in a newspaper, typically including a brief overview of their life and achievements. The notice may also include details about immediate relations, visiting hours and funeral arrangements, such as when and where the ceremony is to be held and whether flowers or donations are appropriate.

Organ donation   The process of removing an organ from one person (donor), living or recently dead, and surgically placing it in a person who needs a transplant (recipient). Many organs can be donated, include the liver, kidney, pancreas and heart. People of all ages may consider themselves potential donors. See also **Body donation**.

Pallbearer   A person who is hired or honoured by the task of helping to carry or officially escort a coffin or casket at a funeral. Family and friends may be asked to carry the coffin. An honorary pallbearer is given special mention but is not required to actually carry the coffin.

Plot   A small piece of ground within a cemetery or graveyard, marked out as a grave. It often contains enough space for several graves which may be shared between family members.

Repatriation   The process of bringing the body of a loved one who died abroad back to their home country or to another country for a funeral or burial.

Tribute   Expressing personal respect or admiration for someone. Traditionally, tribute was material wealth paid by a subject to a ruler. In this context, it denotes a short personal funeral speech that honours one's relationship with the deceased. See also **Homage**.

Undertaker   An alternative word for funeral director.

Urn   A container for cremation ashes, available in many different shapes, materials and styles.

Wake   A watch or vigil held beside the body of someone who has died. Traditional wakes take place at the home of the deceased; modern wakes may be held at a funeral home or another convenient location. Alternatively, a wake is a social gathering associated with death which includes an informal reception with food and drink, or a festive meal, after the funeral service.

RESOURCES

The resources listed below are either books, booklets or informative websites. There are two notes in this section, one that suggests information and tools for dealing with illness and dying and another for bereavement.

CRAFTING RITUAL

Gordon-Lennox, J. (2017) *Crafting Secular Ritual: A Practical Guide.* London & Philadelphia: Jessica Kingsley Publishers.

Gordon-Lennox, J. (ed.) (2017) *Emerging Secular Ritual: A Transdisciplinary Conversation.* London & Philadelphia: Jessica Kingsley Publishers.

FUNERALS/LAST WISHES

Matlins, S.M. (ed.) (2000) *The Perfect Stranger's Guide to Funerals and Grieving Practices.* Woodstock, VT: Skylight Paths Publishing.

Tevlin, K. (2018) 'I Want a Fun Funeral: Putting a Little Life into Your Last Wishes.' Accessed on 31 January 2019 at www.iwantafunfuneral.com

MORTALITY, DEATH AND DYING

Bradley, R. (2016) *A Matter of Life and Death: 60 Voices Share Their Wisdom.* London & Philadelphia: Jessica Kingsley Publishers.

Elfick, H. & Head, D. (2014) *Attending to the Fact – Staying with Dying.* London & Philadelphia: Jessica Kingsley Publishers.

Gawande, A. (2014) *Being Mortal: Illness, Medicine, and What Matters in the End.* London: Profile Books.

Leget, C. (2017) *Art of Living, Art of Dying: Spiritual Care for a Good Death.* London & Philadelphia: Jessica Kingsley Publishers.

NOTES ON MORTALITY, ILLNESS AND DYING

Considering mortality is anxiety provoking for doctors and patients as well as those close to them. Over a thousand years ago, the Greek historian Plutarch (ca. 46–120 CE), who was a contemporary of Pliny the Younger (see Chapter 2), recognized this quandary when he said 'Medicine makes you die longer.'

The aim of healthcare today should be to provide treatment that is consistent with what matters most to the patient. While some people want to do whatever it takes to stay alive as long as possible, others consciously favour a certain quality of life over longevity. The tool below is designed to nourish discussions on expectations, desires and goals.

The first time these questions are raised by an outsider, you – or your patient or doctor – may react by saying, 'That's not relevant right now,' or 'We don't need to think about that.' Even so, the door is now open and the conversation about what wellbeing means has begun. Most people need time to process their feelings and sort out their priorities. Later, they may feel ready and willing to talk about the best way to deal with what they want done – or can do – to ease the last days of life.

ACCOMPANIMENT: GOALS AND PRIORITIES OF AN ILL OR DYING PERSON

1. What is your understanding of your condition today? How do you feel about that now?

2. What might feel troubling to you as you face the future? Remember that it is normal for feelings about one's condition to change.

3. What feels acceptable to you? What might feel to you like an unacceptable sacrifice?

4. With whom do you feel safe? Who do you want to support you?

5. How can we best accompany you in these choices?

As the patient, it is important that you discuss your expectations and desires with those close to you and your healthcare professionals. By identifying and sharing your current goals and priorities for your life, you can work together with the medical team to put into place certain conditions that increase your level of comfort and sense of control. As your situation evolves the answers to these questions may change too.

Patient: My goals and priorities

1. What is my understanding of where I am and of my illness?

2. What are my fears or worries for the future?

3. What are my goals and priorities now?

4. What outcomes are unacceptable to me? What sacrifices am I willing to make? What do I not want to give up?

5. What would a good day look like?

(Adapted from a list proposed
by Atul Gawande, Campbell 2015)

SPEAKING OF DEATH WITH CHILDREN AND YOUTH

Carter, M. (2016) *Helping Children and Adolescents Think about Death, Dying and Bereavement.* London & Philadelphia: Jessica Kingsley Publishers.

Chadwick, A. (2011) *Talking about Death and Bereavement in School: How to Help Children Aged 4 to 11 to Feel Supported and Understood.* London & Philadelphia: Jessica Kingsley Publishers.

Gaines, A.G. & Polsky, M.E. (2017) *I Have a Question about Death: A Book for Children with Autism Spectrum Disorder or Other Special Needs.* London & Philadelphia: Jessica Kingsley Publishers.

Goldman, L. (2009) *Great Answers to Difficult Questions about Death: What Children Need to Know.* London & Philadelphia: Jessica Kingsley Publishers.

Luxmoore, N. (2012) *Young People, Death and the Unfairness of Everything.* London & Philadelphia: Jessica Kingsley Publishers.

Turner, M. (2006) *Talking with Children and Young People about Death and Dying.* London & Philadelphia: Jessica Kingsley Publishers.

BEREAVEMENT

Gersie, A. (1992) *Storymaking in Bereavement: Dragons Fight in the Meadow.* London & Philadelphia: Jessica Kingsley Publishers.

Kauffmann, J.C. & Jordan, M. (2013) *Life after Bereavement: Beyond Tomorrow.* London & Philadelphia: Jessica Kingsley Publishers.

 NOTES ON SOLACE
FOR THE BEREAVED

Great sorrow elicits strong emotions and weakens the body much like a malady. Sad to say, mourners are too often avoided, as though they have caught the plague. Grief is communicable but it does not cause epidemics. Mourners grieve very differently; everyone needs to feel that their friends and family are there for them.

- Write a note to the family to tell them that you are thinking of them in their loss.
- Call or write in the days or weeks after the funeral to let your bereaved friend know that you are thinking of her or him.
- Propose a walk, music, a game or an activity you are used to doing together. Flexible, simple and spontaneous activities are often the best.
- Don't push her or him to talk but don't avoid talking about loss either.
- Take her or him for a meal or for a coffee to show you have not forgotten.
- Don't be hurt if there is no or little response; be gently persistent.
- Send your friend a note or an email on the year anniversary to show you care about this important marker in her or his life.

See also the resources on trauma and healing below.

TRAUMA AND HEALING

Bercelli, D. (2015) *Shake It Off Naturally. Reduce Stress Anxiety and Tension with TRE.* CreateSpace Independent Publishing Platform.

Bercelli's online resources: Tension & Trauma Releasing Exercises. Accessed on 1 February 2019 at https://traumaprevention.com

Haines, S. (2015) *Trauma Is Really Strange.* London & Philadelphia: Singing Dragon.

Haines, S. (2018) *Anxiety Is Really Strange.* London & Philadelphia: Singing Dragon.

Härle, D. (2017) *Trauma-Sensitive Yoga.* London & Philadelphia: Singing Dragon.

Karr-Morse, R. & Wiley, M.S. (2012) *Scared Sick: The Role of Childhood Trauma in Adult Disease.* New York: Basic Books.

Levine, P.A. (2015) *Trauma and Memory: Brain and Body in the Search for the Living Past.* Berkeley, CA: North Atlantic Books.

Somatic Experiencing Trauma Institute (Peter Levine) online resources. Accessed on 1 February 2019 at https://traumahealing.org

REFERENCES

Allison, D.G. (1996) *Two or Three Things I Know for Sure.* London: Penguin Books.

Alpert, B.O. (2020) 'Trauma and Ritual in Prehistory.' In J. Gordon-Lennox (ed.) *Ritual in Fearful Times: An Unexplored Resource for Coping with Trauma.* Charlotte, NC: IAP.

Artigas, L. & Jarero, I. (1998) 'The Butterfly Hug Method for Bilateral Stimulation.' Accessed on 1 February 2019 at http://emdrresearchfoundation.org/toolkit/ butterfly-hug.pdf

Asad, T. (1993) *Genealogies of Religion: Discipline and Reasons of Power in Christianity and Islam.* Baltimore, MD: Johns Hopkins University Press.

Asad, T. (2003) *Formations of the Secular: Christianity, Islam, Modernity.* Cultural Memory in the Present Series. Stanford, CA: Stanford University Press.

Auden, W.H. (1940) *Another Time.* London: Faber & Faber.

Aukeman, A. (2016) *Welcome to Painterland: Bruce Conner and the Rat Bastard Protective Association.* Oakland, CA: University of California Press.

Barrett, L.F. (2017) *How Emotions Are Made: The Secret Life of the Brain.* London: Macmillan.

Bell, A., Jr. (n.d.) 'Who Was Pliny?' Accessed on 1 February 2019 at www.pliny-mysteries.com/who-was-pliny.html

Bell, C. (2009 [1992]) *Ritual Theory, Ritual Practice.* New York: Oxford University Press.

Bell, C. (2009 [1997]) *Ritual: Perspectives and Dimensions.* New York: Oxford University Press.

Bell, C. (n.d.) Believing and the Practice of Religion. Unpublished manuscript, Santa Clara University Library.

Borden, G.P. (2010) 'Preface.' *Material Precedent: Typology of Modern Tectonics.* Hoboken, NJ: John Wiley & Sons.

Bowie, D. (1972) 'My Death.' *Ziggy Stardust and the Spiders from Mars.* EMI. Original French lyrics of 'La Mort' by Jacques Brel (1959).

Bradley, R. (2003) 'A life less ordinary: The ritualization of the domestic sphere in later prehistoric Europe.' *Cambridge Archaeological Journal 13*, 1, 5–23.

Brown, R.M. (1988) 'Introduction.' *Starting from Scratch.* New York: Bantam Books.

Campbell, S. (2015) 'Atul Gawande's 5 Questions to Ask at Life's End.' Next Avenue. Accessed on 1 February 2019 at www.nextavenue.org/blog/ atul-gawande%E2%80%99s-5-questions-ask-life%E2%80%99s-end

Chandernagor, F. (2002) *La Chambre.* Paris: Gallimard.

Chang, S.T. (1986) *The Complete System of Self-Healing: Internal Exercises.* San Francisco, CA: Tao Publishing.

Cohen, A. (ed.) (1991) *The San Francisco Oracle: The Psychedelic Newspaper of the Haight-Ashbury (1966–1968)*. Berkeley, CA: Regent Press.

Corpse Project (2018) 'Can We Lay Bodies to Rest So That They Help the Living and the Earth?' Accessed on 1 February 2019 at www.thecorpseproject.net

De Ville de Goyet, C. (2004) 'Epidemics caused by dead bodies: A disaster myth that does not want to die.' *Pan American Journal Public Health 15*, 5, 297–299.

Dissanayake, E. (1992) *Homo Aestheticus: Where Art Comes From and Why*. New York: Free Press.

Dissanayake, E. (2006) 'The musical impulse.' *Chamber Music 23*, 3, 32–35.

Dissanayake, E. (2017) 'Ethology, interpersonal neurobiology, and play: Insights into the evolutionary origin of the arts.' *American Journal of Play 9*, 2, 143–68.

Economist (2018) 'Making the Reaper Cheaper: Why Undertakers Are Worried.' 12 April. Accessed on 1 February 2019 at www.economist.com/international/2018/04/12/why-undertakers-are-worried

Encyclopaedia Britannica (2018) 'Pliny the Younger, Roman Author.' Accessed on 1 February 2019 at www.britannica.com/biography/Pliny-the-Younger

Evans, J. (2018) 'U.S. Adults are More Religious than Western Europeans.' Pew Research Center. Accessed on 1 February 2019 at www.pewresearch.org/fact-tank/2018/09/05/u-s-adults-are-more-religious-than-western-europeans

Field, C.D. (2011) 'The Ways We Say Goodbye.' 24 January. British Religion in Numbers. Accessed on 1 February 2019 at www.brin.ac.uk/2011/the-ways-we-say-goodbye

Funeral Service Foundation (2012) 'Thoughts and Feelings about Traditional Ceremonies and Your End of Life Ceremony.' Accessed on 1 February 2019 at www.cremationsolutions.com/blog/wp-content/uploads/2014/11/Funeral-Foundation-Study.pdf

Gairin, V. (2010) 'Nouveaux rites. Dossier Pensez la mort: Les textes fondamentaux.' *Le Point Références 1*, 96–7.

Gawande, A. (2011) *The Checklist Manifesto: How to Get Things Right*. New York: Picador.

Geary, P. (1994) *Living with the Dead in the Middle Ages*. Ithaca, NY: Cornell University Press.

Ginsberg, A. (2006) 'Death and Fame.' *Collected Poems, 1947–1997*. New York: HarperCollins.

Grand, D. (2013) *Brainspotting: The Revolutionary New Therapy for Rapid and Effective Change*. Boulder, CO: True Sounds.

Green, J. & Levy, L. (2003) *Jay DeFeo and* The Rose. Berkeley, CA: University of California Press.

Grimes, R.L (2014) Appendices to *The Craft of Ritual Studies*. New York: Oxford University Press. Accessed on 1 March 2019 at http://ronaldlgrimes.twohornedbull.ca/publications/books

Hershkowitz, D. (1995) 'Pliny the poet.' *Greece & Rome xlii*, 2, 168–181.

Holloway, M. (2015) 'Ritual and Meaning-Making in the Face of Contemporary Death.' Keynote lecture, *Symposium: Emerging Rituals in a Transitioning Society.* Utrecht, Netherlands: University of Humanistic Studies.

Hope, V.M. (2009) *Roman Death: The Dying and the Dead in Ancient Rome.* London & New York: Continuum.

Hope, V.M. (2017) 'A Sense of Grief: The Role of the Senses in the Performance of Roman Mourning.' In E. Betts (ed.) *Senses of the Empire: Multisensory Approaches to Roman Culture.* London & New York: Routledge.

Hughes, J.D. (2013) 'Responses to Natural Disasters in the Greek and Roman Worlds.' In K. Pfeifer and N. Pfeifer (eds) *Forces of Nature and Cultural Responses.* Dordrecht: Springer.

Illich, I. (1973) *Tools for Conviviality.* New York: Harper & Row.

Jonte-Pace, D. (2009) 'Foreword.' In C. Bell, *Ritual Theory, Ritual Practice.* New York: Oxford University Press.

Kuhn, T. (1996 [1962]) *The Structure of Scientific Revolution.* Chicago, IL: University of Chicago Press.

Lacombe, U. (2017) *Journey into Sound and into Oneself.* Varanasi: Luminous Books.

Lacy, S. (2019) Website home page. Accessed on 1 March 2019 at http://www.suzannelacy.com

Lenoir, F. (2012) *La Guérison du monde.* Paris: Fayard.

Levine, P.A. (2005) 'Foreword.' In M. Picucci, *Ritual as Resource: Energy for Vibrant Living.* Berkeley, CA: North Atlantic Books.

Levine, P.A. (2010) *In an Unspoken Voice.* Berkeley, CA: North Atlantic Books.

Levine, P.A. (2015) *Trauma and Memory: Brain and Body in a Search for the Living Past.* Berkeley, CA: North Atlantic Books.

Levine, P.A. (2017) Front Matter. In J. Gordon-Lennox (ed.) *Emerging Ritual in Secular Societies: A Transdisciplinary Conversation.* London & Philadelphia: Jessica Kingsley Publishers.

Mandeville-Gamble, S. (2007) 'Guide to the Allen Ginsberg Papers.' Green Library, Department of Special Collections, Stanford University Libraries. Accessed on 1 February 2019 at http://oac.cdlib.org/findaid/ark:/13030/tf5c6004hb

McCrindle (2014) 'Deaths and Funerals in Australia Research Summary.' Accessed on 1 February 2019 at https://mccrindle.com.au/wp-content/uploads/2018/04/Deaths-and-funerals-in-Australia_McCrindle.pdf

Mesquita, B., Boiger, M. & De Leersnyder, J. (2016) 'The cultural construction of emotions.' *Current Opinion in Psychology 8*, 31–36.

Mies van der Rohe, L. (1938) Inaugural address as Director of Architecture at the Armour Institute of Technology, Chicago, IL, 20 November. Papers of Ludwig Mies van der Rohe, Box 61. Manuscript Division, Library of Congress.

Morely, N. (2018) 'Number of Pauper's Funerals Has Shot Up by 12%.' Metro UK. Accessed on 1 February 2019 at https://metro.co.uk/2018/01/17/number-paupers-funerals-shot-12-7236279

Morgan, B. (2007) *I Celebrate Myself: The Somewhat Private Life of Allen Ginsberg.* New York: Penguin.

People's Path (1993) 'Declaration of War Against the Exploiters of Lakota Spirituality.' Accessed on 1 February 2019 at www.thepeoplespaths.net

Pew Research Center (2015) 'The Future of World Religions: Population Growth Projections, 2010–2050.' 2 April. Accessed on 1 February 2019 at www.pewforum.org/2015/04/02/religious-projections-2010-2050/#fn-22652-5

Pliny the Younger (1900 [~104]) *Letters (Epistolae).* Texts modified from translation by W. Melmoth, The Project Gutenberg. Accessed on 30 November 2018 at www.gutenberg.org/files/2811/2811-h/2811-h.htm

Porges, S.W. (2011) *The Polyvagal Theory: Neurophysiologial Foundations of Emotions, Attachment, Communication, and Self-Regulation.* New York: W.W. Norton.

Porges, S.W. (2012) 'Interview with William Stranger at Dharma Cafe.' 6 June. Accessed on 1 February 2019 at https://vimeo.com/44146020

Porges, S.W. (2020) 'Rituals, Contemplative Practices, and Vagal Pathways.' In J. Gordon-Lennox (ed.) *Ritual in Fearful Times: An Unexplored Resource for Coping with Trauma.* Charlotte, NC: IAP.

Remember Me (2018) 'The Changing Face of Memorialization.' Accessed on 1 February 2019 at https://remembermeproject.wordpress.com/the-project

Russo, I. (2017) 'Foreword.' In J. Gordon-Lennox, *Crafting Secular Ritual: A Practical Guide.* London & Philadelphia: Jessica Kingsley Publishers.

Scaer, R.C. (2001) *The Body Bears the Burden.* Philadelphia, PA: Haworth Medical Press.

Scaer, R.C. (2005) *The Trauma Spectrum: Hidden Wounds and Human Resiliency.* New York: W.W. Norton.

Scaer, R.C. (2012) *8 Keys to Body–Brain Balance.* New York: W.W. Norton.

Schnarch, D.M. (1997) *Passionate Marriage: Love, Sex, and Intimacy in Emotionally Committed Relationships.* New York: W.W. Norton.

Seligman, A.B., Weller, R.P., Puett, M. & Simon, B. (2008) *Ritual and Its Consequences: An Essay on the Limits of Sincerity.* New York: Oxford Press.

Shapiro, G. (2013) 'Professor Probes Mental Disorders in the Ancient World.' Columbia News. Columbia University, New York. Accessed on 1 February 2019 at http://news.columbia.edu/content/professor-probes-mental-disorders-ancient-world

Sherwin-White, A.N. (1969) 'Pliny: The Man and His Letters.' *Greece & Rome 16*, 1, 76–90.

Simson, G.W. (1859) 'A Coronach in the Backwoods' (painting). National Museum of Scotland. Accessed on 1 February 2019 at https://artuk.org/discover/artworks/a-coronach-in-the-backwoods-185026

Steinem, G. (2012) 'How I Got into this Room.' *The Humanist.* 18 October. Accessed on 1 February 2019 at http://thehumanist.com/magazine/november-december-2012/features/how-i-got-into-this-room

Stengs, I. (2017) 'Commemorative Ritual and the Power of Place.' In J. Gordon-Lennox (ed.) *Emerging Ritual in Secular Societies.* London & Philadelphia: Jessica Kingsley Publishers.

Stolz, J., Könemann, J., Schneuwly Purdie, M. & Englberger, T. (2011) 'Religiosität in der modernen Welt. Bedingungen, Konstruktionen und sozialer Wandel.' Collectivités religieuses, État et société (PNR 58). Bern: Fonds national suisse (FNS).

SunLife (2015) 'Cost of Dying 2015.' 9 October. Accessed on 1 February 2019 at www. sunlifedirect.co.uk/press-office/cost-of-dying-2015

Tateo, L. (2015) 'Just an illusion? Imagination as higher mental function.' *Journal of Psychology & Psychotherapy 5*, 6. Accessed on 1 February 2019 at www. omicsonline.org/open-access/just-an-illusion-imagination-as-higher-mental-function-2161-0487-1000216.php?aid=65779

Tateo, L. (2016) 'Fear.' In V.P. Glaveanu, L. Tanggaard & C. Wegener (eds) *Creativity – A New Vocabulary.* London: Palgrave Macmillan.

Telegraph Financial Services (2017) 'Alternative and Nonreligious Funeral Services.' Accessed on 1 February 2019 at www.telegraph.co.uk/financial-services/retirement-solutions/funeral-plans/nonreligious-funeral

Tomatis, A.A. (1988) *Les Troubles Scolaires.* Paris: Ergo Press.

Turner Syndrome Society (2018) 'About Turner Syndrome.' Accessed on 1 February 2019 at www.turnersyndrome.org/about-turnersyndrome

Ueland, B. (1938 [2010]) *If You Want to Write.* New York: BN Publishing.

van der Kolk, B.A. (2014) *The Body Keeps the Score: Brain, Mind, and Body in the Healing of Trauma.* New York: Viking Books.

van der Kolk, B.A. (2015) 'Foreword.' In P.A. Levine, *Trauma and Memory: Brain and Body in a Search for the Living Past.* Berkeley, CA: North Atlantic Books.

Van der Lee, I. (2019) Website home page. Accessed on 1 March 2019 at idavanderlee.com

Walker, R. (2003) 'The Guts of a New Machine.' The New York Times. 30 November. Accessed on 1 February 2019 at www.nytimes.com/2003/11/30/magazine/the-guts-of-a-new-machine.html

Zumthor, P. (2006) *Thinking Architecture*, 2nd edn. Basel: Birkhäuser.

INDEX